the Grandpa book II

Editors: *Henry de Fiebre, Jackie Kinney*

Production: *Sally Manich, Sue Flower,
Laura Goodman, Tom LaFleur*

International Standard Book Number: 0-89821-062-3
Library of Congress Catalog Card Number: 82-62527
© 1984, Reiman Publications, Inc.
5400 S. 60th Street, Greendale, Wisconsin 53129
All rights reserved. Printed in U.S.A.

CONTENTS

For This Farmer, There Could Only Be One Dog!

By Martha Sweeney

Most any nice afternoon, the seasoned old farmer can be found sitting in a rusty springsteel chair under the shade of a huge hackberry tree. His farm is quiet now...but, as always, the black-and-white border collie sits attentively beside him, ever ready to obey her master's command.

"Good dog," 88-year-old Alfred Kusenberger murmurs as he strokes the dog's head. And as he pets the dog...he remembers.

* * * * * * *

Peggy first came to Alfred's small stock farm near Stonewall in the Texas hill country as a pup more than 20 years ago. "I trained her myself," Alfred says. "She was so smart, she could herd sheep better than any dog you ever saw."

For half a dozen years, they worked side by side every day. Then late one night a neighbor knocked on Alfred's door. He had found Peggy—dead—on the main road a half mile from the farm.

Alfred was heartbroken. It didn't seem possible that Peggy would no longer greet him each morning, making the odd throaty sound she always made when she was happy. For days, as he dozed in his springsteel chair, he thought he could feel her cold-nosed muzzle wiggle into his hand...but when he opened his eyes he knew she was gone.

Alfred's wife, Aminda, suggested they get another dog, but Alfred wouldn't hear of it. Finally, though, to please his wife, he agreed to look at a litter of border collie pups. Alfred showed no interest in the bouncing pups at the sale...but one female kept pawing at the wire in front of his feet so hard that Aminda finally picked her out to take home.

On the way back to the farm, Alfred indifferently held the puppy in his lap without as much as looking at her. Then the puppy made an odd, throaty sound...just like Peggy had. Alfred's heart jumped. "Peggy?" he said, cuddling the pup to him. "You sure sound like her." Aminda gave a silent sigh of relief.

Soon it was just like old times on the farm. "It was as if she already knew her way around," Alfred says of the second Peggy. "She never even explored the place. She just went to the doghouse I'd built for Peggy and settled down, like she'd been living there for years!"

And like her predecessor, this Peggy was a hard worker. "All I'd have to do was say 'Get the sheep, Peggy' and she'd tear off to the

"PEGGY" has been a loyal companion to Alfred (left) for years—this unusual story shows how strong the bond between a farmer and his dog can grow!

pasture and bring them up to the corral by herself. And she was just as good with cattle," Alfred says proudly.

It seemed Peggy feared only one thing, and that was thunder.

"Peggy always followed me out into the field every morning and ran beside the tractor," Alfred recalls with a pained look in his eyes. "But one day she was acting so funny I had to stop the tractor to see what the matter was. That's when I heard the thunder in the distance."

Peggy and Alfred raced for home, and had no sooner put the tractor under the shed than a big storm broke. Peggy made a dive for her doghouse as Alfred ran into the house.

When the storm had passed, Peggy was *gone.* Alfred searched his farm for her, to no avail. He ran ads on the radio and in newspapers, and received calls from as far as 30 miles away, but the calls never led to Peggy. Finally, heartsick, he accepted the fact she must be dead.

As the days wore on, Alfred became more sick with grief. "No, no," he told Aminda when she'd try to raise the subject. "No more dogs. You needn't talk about it."

But with Alfred in his 80's, Aminda knew they would need help with the livestock. So when she heard a neighbor had a young dog available, she went alone to look. Like the two Peggies, this dog had the typical black-and-white markings of the border collie—but it was part Australian sheep dog…and it was a male.

"Maybe," Aminda thought to herself, "it's best not to have another Peggy." She took the dog home and put it in Alfred's arms—and immediately the dog made the familiar odd throaty sound his two predecessors had.

"Peggy!" Alfred said, surprised.

"No, no," Aminda said firmly. "Alfred, you can't call this dog 'Peggy'. It's a he. And, besides, I've already named him 'Tippy'. Don't you think that's a good name?"

"Sure," Alfred replied agreeably. "Tippy's a good name."

* * * * * * *

Tippy is still Alfred's constant companion, all these years later. But no one ever calls him Tippy anymore.

Now, as Alfred rises from his springsteel chair to see a visitor off, he says to the dog, "Come on, we've got a lot of work to do…*Peggy!*"

He winks mischievously at his wife as he pronounces the name. Aminda just laughs as she shakes her head at her husband, thoughts of ever persuading Alfred to call a dog anything but "Peggy" long forgotten.

And as Alfred and Peggy walk off toward the livestock, the dog happily lifts its soft, brown eyes to its master—and makes an odd throaty sound.

His New England Farm's The Grandpa of Them All

By Trish Valicenti of Montreal, Quebec, Canada

Hugh Tuttle, like all farmers, wakes every morning long before dawn—he has to hurry to make sure all is well on his 60 acres that grow more than 300 kinds of fruits and vegetables.

But Hugh differs from other farmers in one way—the land he lovingly cares for is the *oldest* farm in America!

A Tuttle has tilled this same soil in Dover, New Hampshire for more than 350 years, since Angel Gabriel Tuttle crossed the Atlantic from England in 1632 and established the farm.

Hugh, 62, is the 10th generation of Tuttles—direct descendants of Angel Gabriel—to work the farm. The Tuttles were Quakers, Hugh explains, and tradition for years dictated that the youngest son inherit the farm. (The oldest son was expected to make his own way.)

Hugh, himself, was the youngest son in his family—but he dreamed of becoming a doctor, not a farmer.

As a young man, he left the family farm, 7 miles from the New Hampshire shoreline, to study medicine at Harvard, an hour away in Cambridge, Massachusetts.

But the pull of the farm was strong.

"I can't really explain it," Hugh says, thoughtfully, "but one morning I was walking across the yard at Harvard on a bright spring day, and I was suddenly struck by a tremendous desire to be back on the farm."

So Hugh packed his bags, bid Harvard good-bye and returned to Dover...content to take care of vegetables rather than sick people.

"My vegetables don't seem to mind that I don't have a degree," Hugh chuckles.

Hugh eventually took over the farm and since has worked "8 days a week". He's proud of his land, and a visitor gets a long tour over the dirt roads encircling the farm that grows the famous Tuttle vegetables.

"I can tell which rows I planted myself," Hugh says with pride, as he stares at newly planted peas in a small plot. "They're the *straight* ones."

Hugh, with the help of a daughter and several full-time employees, does all the planting on the farm. In the summer, he hires about 50 agricultural students from the nearby state university to help with harvesting, washing and packaging the produce.

Every vegetable imaginable is grown on the Tuttle farm, with greenhouses aiding in early germination and planting. Flowering and non-flowering plants and cut flowers are also cash crops for Hugh—he's hired a young couple whose specialty is horticulture to oversee that operation.

Among all the vegetables he grows, Hugh admits to a fondness for asparagus. "It's a fussy crop," he explains. And strawberries are a longtime Tuttle specialty...Hugh confesses that he grows a private stock of the fruit just for family consumption.

The soil on the Tuttle farm is a combina-

SPECIAL soil fills Hugh Tuttle's hands...it's part of the land Hugh and his ancestors have farmed since 1632!

tion of loam, clay, silt and sand. The land, according to Hugh, is one of the few tillable spots in the extreme southeast section of New Hampshire.

While Hugh has a healthy respect for the past, he is not afraid to make changes on the farm when they seem necessary. For example, he planted pine trees on part of his property for the first time this year—when they're sold later as Christmas trees, they'll provide one more source of income for the family farm.

Hugh's also introduced a Japanese farming technique—terracing—to maximize space for growing crops.

The Tuttle farm used to be famous for supplying local grocers with the freshest vegetables around. But in 1957 the family barn was converted into a roadside fruit and vegetable stand—and that's now grown into a three-room, retail produce store.

People come from all over the country to shop at the store—and then tell their friends back home they bought their vegetables and fruit at the oldest farm in the country!

It is a small plot nestled among maples that Hugh believes was the beginning of the farm 350 years ago. Imbued with the history of his farm, Hugh decided a couple years ago to find out firsthand what it was like to be an early settler like his ancestor Angel Gabriel.

"I cleared that plot of land myself and planted alternating crops of buckwheat and winter rye," Hugh says, shaking his head in admiration. "I'll tell you, I don't know how those early settlers did it. All they knew about farming was what the Indians told them…and there was no convenient farm supply store up the road!"

While Hugh has modern farming tools Angel Gabriel couldn't even have dreamed of in 1632, it's no secret that his key to success is plain, old hard work. He finishes his chores about 6 p.m. each day and is never in bed later than 8 p.m.

Hugh and his wife, Joan, now live in a small house on the farm—they used to live in the 200-year-old, eight-room Colonial that's the farm's main house…but their son, William Penn "Bill" Tuttle III, lives there now with his wife and two small children.

Just like his father, Bill left Dover as a young man with no intention of ever taking over the farm. He studied sociology at Tufts Univ. in Medford, Massachusetts, and Hugh thought his son would never return.

"Then, early one afternoon, Bill came back to the farm and said, 'Dad, how would you like to hire a good man?' " Hugh recalls with a warm smile.

Bill has turned out to be a good man… and more. The family farm store sells fresh fruits and vegetables year round, even when it can't be filled with Tuttle vegetables. That's because Bill leaves Dover every morning at 2 o'clock to buy the freshest produce at the farm market in Boston.

Bill will take over the farm someday, according to Hugh. But there's a new twist to the father-to-son passage of the land.

Hugh's two daughters, Becky and Lucy, both also left the farm when they were young, then returned. Now the daughters also live there with their families. Becky helps her dad with planting, while Lucy—who calls herself the "front-room Tuttle"—works in the retail store.

"This is a four-family farm now," Hugh says. "I know it's a break with tradition, having the daughters share in its operation—but the most important thing to me is seeing that this farm continues as a family farm."

Perhaps for *another* 350 years…

TELLTALE SIGN. "I know which rows I planted," Hugh says. "They're the straight ones!"

Iowa Farmers Keep Busy Milling Around

By Warren Jacobsen and Judy Sutcliffe

This story began when Iowa farmer Harvey Sornson returned from a visit to Denmark with a gleam in his eye.

Harvey had a wild, wonderful idea...but he wasn't sure how his American Danish friends and neighbors back home in western Iowa would react to it.

Ever since a childhood visit to his parents' native Denmark, Harvey had been fascinated with the big windmills dotting Denmark's countryside. On his most recent trip back to Denmark, Harvey noticed that the old windmills were gradually disappearing—most of them hadn't been used to grind wheat for a long time, and many were more than 100 years old.

To Harvey, those windmills were symbols of his rural Danish heritage. "I thought I'd like to take one home to Iowa," he says.

Harvey's farm near Elk Horn, Iowa is in the center of one of this country's largest Danish settlements. Like Harvey, his Danish-American neighbors treasure their heritage. Many of them still speak Danish and eat kringle (a Danish pastry) and open-faced sandwiches.

Back home, Harvey first tried out his idea on just a few friends and neighbors.

"They didn't take my idea seriously," he recalls. " 'Bring a Danish mill over here?' they exclaimed. 'You're crazy, Harvey. Besides, it's impossible!' "

But Harvey isn't one to give up easily—he's one of those so-called "stubborn Danes".

Harvey's idea got a big boost when cousins of another Elk Horn resident, Milo Andersen, came from Denmark for a visit. "They soon heard about the windmill plan," Harvey explains, and when they returned home, they scouted around for a windmill for Elk Horn.

They found one in a few weeks...but the 127-year-old mill would cost about $33,000, including ocean freight to America.

That's a lot of money, but by the time the mill had been located, Harvey's idea had caught on like wildfire. In a matter of days, residents of the small Danish community had pledged the money needed to move the windmill.

Only 5 months after Harvey came up with his wild idea, carpenters in Denmark took the old mill down. As they worked, they made a scale model with each piece numbered to correspond to the actual mill—this would be the only "instruction sheet" for reassembling the mill in Iowa.

If the Iowa Danes could manage to fit all the pieces of the giant puzzle back together, they'd be rewarded with an authentic Danish windmill 60 feet high, with wings 66 feet long. Eighty shutters lining the wings would catch the wind, turn the gears and grind the grain against the millstone.

The mill finally arrived in Iowa as two truckloads of timbers and gears. "One of the truck drivers told us we'd never get it put back together," Harvey recalls with a grin.

DREAM FULFILLED. *Old Danish windmill is at home among cornfields, thanks to farmer's dream.*

But every day, dozens of volunteer workers, mostly farmers and retired farmers, showed up at the mill's new location at the end of Elk Horn's main street.

Reconstruction of the mill took nearly a year, and Harvey was on hand to give the official "countdown" over a loudspeaker on a cold November day when the two 3,500-lb. crossbars were hoisted into place. Hundreds of spectators cheered when the big job was done.

"Now it looks like a windmill," Harvey said with a satisfied smile. His dream had become the dream of an entire town...and the dream had come true.

Today, Elk Horn's Danish windmill is a proud reminder of the town's Danish heritage... and of the determination of some American farmers who are also "stubborn Danes".

Dakota Farmer's Life Is a Long Open Book

By Lorraine Ode of Mumford, New York

On February 17, 1913, the weather turned unexpectedly warm on the prairies of South Dakota. The day was so springlike, in fact, that Peder Phillips' brother, Ben, became "antsy"...and decided to get a head start on disking the cornstalks. To Peder, then 19, this small event seemed worthy of note. And since that day, nothing that's happened on the family's Valley Springs, South Dakota farm has gone unnoticed—or unnoted—by Peder.

Beginning with that warm February day some 70 years ago, Peder has found time to make daily notations on the weather and his activities for each day. He calls the resulting 25-volume, handwritten history "a diary of the common man".

Peder retired recently after a lifetime of growing corn, wheat and soybeans and raising cattle and sheep. Through those long years of farming, he formed his own ideas about history.

History, Peder observes, is usually told in terms of "mountains and valleys"—the highs and lows of life—with plateaus only rarely being noted. But, he points out, much of the common man's life is spent on plateaus—chopping wood ...visiting relatives...going to funerals...pausing for a sunset. "What bugs me so much about history," he says with sureness, in an accent that unmistakably reveals his Norwegian ancestry, "is that so many people don't see the simple things."

The simple things—none of them are missing from Peder's history. Take any of Peder's 25 volumes off the shelf, open it up and you will find a description of what makes up the day-to-day life of a farmer...any farmer.

It's all there—the death of a favorite horse, chores, weddings, how the crops are doing. The prose is sometimes terse, sometimes sentimental...a farmer's life on paper.

Turn to August 13, 1914. That's the day Valley Springs suffered through a hailstorm so severe that the hail balls cut the hide of horses

LIVELY STORY fills Peder Phillips' diary—he started it at 19, and has written on every day since!

9

A VERY GOOD YEAR! Peder's diary records a bumper crop of cabbages in 1915—350 of them!

Diary...

as they huddled in the pasture.

December 13, 1938 had none of that excitement. The weather was "raw and inclined to be a little snowy". Peder towed logs most of the day.

More recently, on February 14, 1981, Peder wrote, "The early dawning in kaleidoscope colors caused a sparse snow near the house to become pinkish from the reflection."

To Peder Phillips, all that is worth remembering...and recording.

August 24, 1964: "...I accompanied the trucker to the pasture where Broncho had died. Gives a fellow a sad feeling to see a faithful horse trucked away in death..."

May 13, 1924: "Rain, sleet and snow. Bad day. It seemed unreasonable to see farmers planting corn with snow scooting around them."

Peder's fascination with birds colors much of his writing. A recent summer's mild weather brought many Southern birds farther north, and his sighting of a scarlet tanager—unusual for South Dakota—brought a soft chuckle.

"Seeing that tanager," Peder wrote, "did more for me than drinking a gallon of whiskey."

There are now some 25,000 entries in Peder's diary—one for each day of each year for more than 70 years. And each entry begins with what you might expect from a dyed-in-the-wool farmer: a description of the weather.

A High Plains farmer like Peder just naturally grows up with one eye on the sky—

what's up there is more important than anything else.

Consider Peder's entry for September 11, 1930: "Foggy this morning," he began in writing of that day. "A very fine day. Nice and warm with a south wind."

It was only after recording those important details that Peder got around to mentioning something else that happened that day—he got married!

Through the years, Peder's been tempted several times to abandon his daily record. Once, returning from action overseas in World War I, he became seasick. But he kept the events of each day in his head until he was well and able to commit them to paper.

"To tell the truth," he admits, "it takes a lot of gumption to keep something like this up for so long. But if you once start letting it go, you kill the whole idea of it."

Peder plans to keep making his daily diary entry as long as he's able. Even now, the first thing he does every morning is write down the weather and events of the day before.

Now that he's recorded 70 years in the life of a farmer, Peder is beginning to wonder what to do with his unique history. Several people have contacted him about having his diary published as a book, but he's not so sure...he kept it mostly for himself, and he thinks it means more in his own handwriting.

Likewise, a university has asked to take over the books for safekeeping—"I do worry about losing my books to fire here," Peder says.

Still, he's reluctant to part with them. "If I gave them to the college," he says, "I wouldn't be able to read them whenever I like as I do now."

So, for the time being at least, the 25 bound volumes will remain right on Peder's farm. There, from time to time, Peder will pick one up, open to a page—and relive the uncommon memories of a common man.

Horse Needs Tune-Up?

THE OLD-TIME blacksmith had it all over today's auto serviceman. When you used to take your horse to a blacksmith to be shod, he didn't come up with a dozen other things that had to be fixed!

—*Charles L. Baird*
Maryville, Missouri

Joe and Ernie: They're A Couple of Good Eggs!

By Karen Engle of Long Prairie, Minnesota

A dozen eggs for 7¢ and 10¢? You won't find those prices at Easter anymore, but Joe and Ernie Kreemer well remember such charges for eggs at Kreemers Produce, the country shop they've been operating at Osakis, Minnesota for half a century.

Brother Joe started the business in 1933—today it's still going strong. Kreemers is the only place left where area farmers can drop off a case of eggs or a customer can choose between white and brown eggs.

Joe, 80, remembers opening the shop on June 28, 1933. Brother Ernie, who's 69, joined him 2 years later.

Joe's brother-in-law was skeptical and predicted the business wouldn't last. North American, a competitor that operated a cream station in town, was already well-established.

"Those were the days when everybody raised chickens," Joe recalls. He started the business with the backing of several friends and the Litchfield Produce Co.

"Whenever North American offered farmers a few cents more for eggs," he says, "I'd phone Litchfield and ask 'em what to do. They'd say, 'Beat 'em, beat 'em!' So I would raise our price a little."

The first shop started in an old livery building which burned in 1935. The present 32- x 36-ft. structure was then built to replace it. "We're the oldest business in town," Joe notes with pride.

In the 1930's, eggs sold for 7¢ and 10¢ a dozen, and there were only two grades, Joe points out. The eggs Joe and Ernie bought were first shipped to Litchfield and later to Melrose, where all the inspecting and candling was done.

The heyday of the egg business was the '40's and '50's, when a dozen eggs brought as much as 60¢. In those days almost all area

MIGHTY "HANDY". *Customers at Joe and Ernie's still hand-select small eggs for 25¢/dozen. Right, Ernie sorts and packs.*

"EGGS-PERTS". Joe and Ernie know eggs "inside and out". In summer they chat with customers outside their market, and in winter they gather near the stove to warm up with local gossip. They've been in the business so long they remember when eggs sold for 7¢ and 10¢ a dozen! Their busiest day ever saw 100 cases arrive.

Eggs...

farmers had flocks of 200 to 500 chickens, laying 300 or more eggs a day. The brothers often found themselves scurrying across the wooden-planked floor from the back room where the eggs were stored to the old cash register that even now still rings and pops up dollar and cent amounts on white metal tabs.

"Those were good days for us," sighs Joe, tucking his hands inside his "Big Smith" overalls. "Farmers brought in eggs from all over." The Kreemers often handled 50 to 70 cases a day—with each case holding 360 eggs.

Both brothers remember their busiest day. "It was the day after New Year's back during that period and we'd been closed for a couple of days," Joe remembers. "More than 100 cases came in that day."

In those days, Kreemers Produce opened at 7 a.m., 6 days a week. "We still open at 7," Joe says, "except when it's really cold out. Then we might stretch it to 8."

The brothers handled more than eggs back in the early days. Until 10 years ago, they also sold old hens. An old, hooked chicken catcher still hangs above the shop's stove. "Whenever someone wants to catch a few

chickens, we let them borrow it," chuckles Joe.

The Kreemers also sold machinery and feed—New Idea and Minnesota spreaders, plows, rakes and other small equipment—for some 20 years.

Today, their merchandise—other than eggs—is down to a "few odds and ends". A few Surge inflations and brushes line one shelf, and a Tom Moore ginger ale bottle labeled "blossom set" sits in a glass case with other "remedies and rat poisons".

On an upper shelf sit old egg slips in boxes, alongside receipts and income tax returns. At one time, the brothers also bought and sold cream from farmers.

A few old wooden cases and cardboard boxes line one wall. In a corner, a fishing reel and minnow pail reveal Ernie's favorite pastime. He also has a garden out back, as well as one at home. Every fall, customers anxiously wait for Ernie to get out an old metal egg pail filled with his specialty, Spanish onions.

These days, the brothers buy eggs from only about a dozen farmers, and Joe blames the large egg producers for making the egg business unprofitable for small farmers. Eggs today don't bring much more than in the '50's, he says—Kreemers' price for large white and brown eggs is 65¢ a dozen.

Both brothers chuckle when asked about the difference between white and brown eggs. They'll tell you that people back East prefer brown eggs...but there really is no difference, except perhaps that the brown variety is better for boiling.

The brothers still sell poultry grit and oyster shells and, if they hunt hard enough, there is an old water drinker around someplace. A message on a blackboard reads, "For Sale: 150 one-year-old hens, $1 each."

Times may change, but not Kreemers Produce. People still bring their own cartons most of the time when picking up eggs. The Kreemers know nearly all of their customers personally and visit with them while packing egg orders.

Shortly after 5:30 p.m. each day, Ernie puts on his cap and heads for home. Joe, wanders back to his kitchen in the back of the shop to start a few things for supper.

One thing for sure, no matter what else might change, the brothers need never worry about running out of eggs for themselves.

"If it looks like we're going to run short," Joe confides with a sly twinkle in his eye, "I just stash a few away!"

Weather or Not...This Farmer Can Tell You!

By Randall Howell of Aberdeen, South Dakota

On Christmas Eve each year, 64-year-old Wilbur Hefti sits down at his kitchen table and goes to work.

He has to—his friends and neighbors in northeastern Nebraska have come to rely on Wilbur to tell them when to plant their corn and beans each spring.

Wilbur, of rural Carroll, Nebraska, is a lifelong farmer, not a meteorologist. But since the 1940's, this livestock producer and horse breeder has been annually predicting how much moisture will fall in Wayne County and its environs.

Does he use some fancy weather-tracking machine to make his forecasts? Not Wilbur—to him, the key is onions.

Onions? You bet...six of them, to be exact! They're the biggest part of a time-honored Swiss tradition of weather forecasting that's been handed down to Wilbur through several generations.

Wilbur's forecasts don't tell you how cold or warm a certain day will be—they're limited strictly to moisture, and the prediction is month-to-month, not day-to-day. But to Wilbur and his neighbors, moisture (or its lack) counts for most of the weather.

And so area farmers count on Wilbur. "Friends and neighbors are always asking me what the onions said for this month or the next," he beams. "And, believe me, they give it to me plenty if I'm wrong!"

But Wilbur hasn't been wrong often. His yearly forecasts consistently turn out to be 60% to 80% accurate.

Wilbur learned the forecasting technique from his full-blooded Swiss father, and he's never deviated from it.

The forecasting ritual must take place on Christmas Eve between 11 p.m. and midnight, the hour—centuries of Swiss faith hold—that Christ was born. All it takes are some common household items combined with signs of the Christian faithful.

"You need six onions and a knife," Wilbur explains. The onions—regular, large cooking onions, about the size of a man's fist—are placed on a tabletop and cut lengthwise.

The cutting of the six onions produces a dozen onion halves, each representing one of the 12 months of the coming year. "Then you have to pop the core out, leaving only the outer two rings," Wilbur adds. "The rings form cups."

After the onion "cups" are lined up along the tabletop and each given—in sequence—the name of a month, about 3/4 of a teaspoon of non-iodized salt is dumped into each one.

"You say the three holy names (Father, Son and Holy Ghost) over each one as you dump the salt into them," Wilbur points out. Finally, with a silent hand gesture, Wilbur makes the sign of the cross over the lineup of onion cups.

That's all there is to it, Wilbur says. The

SNOW FOOLIN'! Wilbur Hefti wasn't surprised when a blizzard covered his Nebraska farm—he knew a full month earlier it was going to happen!

onion cups remain in the kitchen, untouched until morning.

"They can be left longer, if you want," Wilbur allows, "but I always check them first thing in the morning."

Where does the weather prediction come from? "In the morning," Wilbur says, "some of the onions will be real watery, some damp, and in others the salt will be just as dry as when I put it in there. I've seen the salt be bone-dry

FARMER'S FORECAST involves slicing six onions, then pouring salt into each half.

when I dump it out...and I've seen onions so wet that the water runs out onto the tabletop."

It's the moisture Wilbur finds in the onion—or the lack of it—that forms the weather prediction for the month that has been assigned to the onion.

Christmas Eve weather predicting has been a ritual in the Hefti family as far back as Wilbur can remember. He especially recalls Christmas of 1935, when his father was still performing the ritual.

"The onions assigned for the summer months you could dump all the salt right out of," he remembers. "They were bone-dry."

It turned out that the 1936 crop season, indeed, was one of the area's driest. "I cut corn with horses and a binder right after the Fourth of July that year," Wilbur says. "It was only hip-high...almost nothing there."

Wilbur is the first to admit that the onions are not always right. "But then, nothing's 100% sure," he notes. "Still, with the onions, you're just about able to tell if you're going to have a crop next year or not, right there on Christmas Eve."

The one thing Wilbur takes pains to point out is that his predictions apply only to his immediate area. Forecasters elsewhere, he says, need to learn the ritual themselves and call their own weather shots.

And, he adds with a smile, they have to watch their technique, too.

"My sister tried the onion ritual one year," he laughs, "but she cut them the wrong way. That left a hole in the bottom—and all the water just ran out!"

'Andy' Anderson: He's a Character—Just Like Ole!

By Tom LaFleur

Andy Anderson has been provoking smiles and laughter from his friends and neighbors in Lindsborg, Kansas for a long while now. He's 95 now...and still going strong!

Andy (Clarence is his real name) believes in living life to the fullest, and he tries to bring that same zest to other folks' lives, as well. Here are just a few examples:

● In the hot summer of 1980, the temperature in Kansas topped 100° for several days in a row. That was no problem for Andy, though—he simply went swimming in the Lindsborg city pool! You can bet he was the only 90-plus citizen in the water.

● Swimming's not Andy's only talent. Not long ago, he sang a Swedish song at his church's talent fair.

● Back when he was a "youngster" of 80, Andy brought home a typewriter and taught himself to type. He had a book in mind...but more of that later.

● In his early farming days, Andy purchased the first tractor in his part of Ness County. And what other farmer do you know who loads up his wagon with a ton of watermelons and gives them away to schoolchildren? Andy did just that for 17 years. And in the rare years when his crop of melons failed, he scoured the countryside and bought melons so no child would be disappointed.

When you meet Andy, you never forget his twinkling eyes and broad smile...and you're captivated by the endless selection of "tall tales" he amuses you with—mostly featuring himself and a character named "Ole", an imaginary hired hand.

It was these tall tales that Andy wanted to collect in a book—and did, in 1972. Sometimes it's difficult to tell where the real world of Clarence Anderson ends and the imaginary world of Andy and Ole begins.

We do know that the real life of Andy Anderson has been lived close to the soil and has deep roots.

Clarence's Swedish immigrant grandfather homesteaded 80 acres near Lindsborg in central Kansas. Clarence's father, John, eventually turned the farm into a veritable truck garden, for which Clarence became the chief salesman. Shy by nature, he was forced to do a lot of talking. He readily admits, "I've been talking ever since!"

In 1915, lured by reports of rich farmland at $15, Andy and brother Philip left for western Kansas to "make their fortune". The first year was lean, and they mostly subsisted on potatoes, cocoa and crackers. Their last $10 bill, hidden in the barn loft for safekeeping, was chewed up by mice. A discouraged Philip returned home.

Andy, however, held on. The second year on the farm brought a 30-bushel-yield crop, and Andy was able to purchase that tractor we mentioned earlier. In 1920, he bought a farm near Utica in Lane County...and also took a bride, Helen Brocher of Beeler, Kansas. They had five children and eventually acquired 15 quarter sections of land.

ACTIVE ANDY. Age hasn't slowed Andy down—he still loves to spin yarns...and to cool off in city pool!

In 1962, Andy and Helen "came home" to Lindsborg and the small farm homesteaded by his grandfather. The farm is adjacent to Bethany College, and Andy can look across the acreage and see students playing on Anderson Field, bequeathed to the college by his brother Philip. Andy enjoys being close to so many young people...he says it's one of the things that keeps *him* young.

Soon after moving back to Lindsborg, he

began his yearly gift of melons. Why did he do it? "I just plain *like* people," says Andy with a gentle smile.

"People like him, too," adds daughter Aleda Schreiber who, with her two children, has lived with and cared for her father since she was widowed in 1973. "His birthday parties are attended by scores of friends...which tells something about how folks feel."

How Andy feels about people is perhaps best described by this true story. One day the local banker phoned Andy and told him he needed to put some money in his checking account that very day. Andy replied that his wife was away and he was too busy in the fields to come to town, but that he'd somehow get the money to the bank before it closed.

Late in the afternoon, a stranger approached the banker and said he'd been flagged down by a farmer as he drove along the road. The farmer had thrust $100 into the startled man's hands and asked him to deposit it in the bank! The stranger, however, had forgotten the farmer's name.

The banker laughed and said, "That has to be Clarence Anderson."

"Yes, that's the name," the stranger agreed—and handed over the $100.

Asked about this episode, Andy chuckles. "Yes, that actually happened...and I'd do it again! I'd rather be hurt once in a while for trusting people than wither and dry up by not trusting them."

Then he asks if we've heard the story about Ole and the Pot of Gold. When we shake our head "no", he begins:

"There's a pot of gold at the end of the rainbow. The only problem is getting to it before the rainbow disappears. This is how Ole did it.

"We know that a rainbow recedes as you approach it. So, to fool the rainbow, Ole held up a mirror and stalked the rainbow by looking in the mirror and walking *backwards*. He sneaked close enough to find and get the gold. You see, the rainbow thought Ole was walking *away* ...and did not recede as usual."

Andy's been entertaining folks with Ole stories for years. If you liked the Pot of Gold story, you'll probably enjoy the other 43 tales in Andy's book, *The Adventures of Ole and Andy*. It's available from Mrs. Aleda Schreiber, 800 N. Kansas St., Lindsborg KS 67456. Cost is $3 plus 65¢ for postage and handling.

Farming...Families...Females: Texan Has Plenty To Say!

By Diane K. Gentry

He's harvested this year's hay crop the same way he harvested his first 81 years ago—walking behind a team of mules.

Bruce Crayton was just 8 years old when his father strapped him to the plow shaft with his belt so the mules on their small Texas farm wouldn't get away from him. He's 89 now—and they've yet to get away from him.

Like his daddy, Bruce grew up "a plain country boy", working farms and ranches all across Texas.

"I never thought about bein' nothin' but a farmer," says Bruce, who, along with his "little" brother Baylor, 87, raises a few hogs and grows 40 acres of hay, corn and sugarcane.

"Daddy was always strict about us workin' the land," he continues. "He said farming was better fer us...better fer the country, too. We'd be in a real fix if all we had was bookkeepers and bankers!"

The land Bruce and his brother have worked for 54 years is the last small island of tranquility in a sea of suburbs surrounding the nearby city of San Marcos, Texas. There are plush homes up on the hills behind their place, where doctors and lawyers lob tennis balls on private courts.

"I wouldn't spend a single day workin' in the city like those folks do," Bruce asserts. "That ain't no place for anybody who thinks anything of himself. The man who works the fields and gets all the fresh air is healthy like me."

Developers with cash-register eyes come calling on Bruce often. The Crayton brothers' small farm could be divided up into nearly 100 choice lots worth hundreds of thousands of dollars.

Bruce just smiles at them, shakes his head …and goes right on farming.

"There's too many people around here already," he says. "I like my old house, and I'm proud of my old mules. I believe the simple life is one of the sweetest things a body can have—makes me sad to see the whole world goin' to money.

"A rich man," Bruce adds with a shrug, "goes out the same as a poor man when his time comes. I reckon I ain't gonna have too much to carry with me."

Those anxious developers would shudder if they knew how easily Bruce and Baylor acquired their farm back in 1930. "Baylor traded a sorrel mare and $40 for this place," Bruce explains.

With a grin he adds, "But the other feller had to whup him first to convince him to trade!"

Baylor snorts. He's quick to point out the difference between him and his big brother. "I am an *educated* man," Baylor says. (He finished the sixth grade; Bruce never ventured inside a schoolhouse.) "I believe in tractors," Baylor adds, "but Bruce here only believes in mules."

Since Bruce does all the fieldwork, there isn't a tractor on the place—just 12 hungry mules.

Sometimes the slowness of the mules irritates Baylor. Once when Bruce was "loggin'" (dragging a log behind a mule team to level the ground), Baylor bounced his 1959 Pontiac into

HE'S MULE-ISH! In 80 years of farming, Bruce has never used a tractor. "Mules were made for work like this," he explains.

the field with a log tied to the back bumper and logged off 20 acres in 45 minutes.

"I told him he did an all right job," Bruce admits. "But anything done that fast can't be real good.

"Mules were made for work like that," Bruce insists. "An idle mule is the devil's playground.

"Daddy sold mules to farmers all over this country, and he learnt me how to break 'em. I can jest catch a wild mule and tie him to a tree. Next I hitch him right up next to a gentle mule, an' he's broke."

Long before suburbs began sprouting up all around him, Bruce used his mules to dig stock ponds for neighboring farmers. He'd appear at the site with 16 mules to cut, scrape and haul the dirt for a 140-ft.-long, 40-ft.-wide, 8-ft.-deep pond.

"I can tell you this—any pond I ever built still holds water today," he asserts.

Bruce loves to reminisce about his family's role in taming the American West, tracing his origins with a colorful if somewhat less-than-accurate grasp of history:

"My grandmother was a Cherokee In-dian," he explains, "who was captured by my grandfather, Old Man Crayton, about the time Christopher Columbus discovered America.

"Now this Columbus fella, he was 3 months gettin' here in one of those old-timey boats," Bruce continues with a sweep of his arm. "Everyone else on the boat gave up on finding land, but ol' Columbus…'Bound to be land somewhere!' he told 'em.

"Then one evening a dove flew up to the boat with a stick in her mouth—land ahead! Columbus pulled the boat up and tied it on the back side of the world somewhere.

"I'll tell you," Bruce adds with authority, "America was a wild place back then. There were only Indians here—my kinfolk—and panthers, bears and Arabian horses."

Bruce's accounts of more recent history are no less intriguing…and a bit more credible. His parents, he says, were married in the middle of a road, surrounded by 3,000 head of cattle.

"Daddy was on his way to Kansas with them cattle," he says, "and he knew it'd be 3 months before he saw Mama again. So he married her on the spot before leaving. Daddy worked hard drivin' cattle all across the country to support Mama and us kids."

Bruce firmly believes that the old days of

his boyhood were vastly superior to anything modern progress has to offer. Family ties were strong back then, Bruce points out, in spite of his father's long absences. "There was 18 of us kids—nine boys and nine girls—and there wasn't a woods colt among us," he says. ("A woods colt," he explains, "is a wild one that doesn't know its daddy. We all knew ours.")

"Mama stayed home cooking," Bruce continues. "I never went to the table in my life when it wasn't set all pretty with a cloth on it and plumb full up with food."

As far as Bruce is concerned, farming isn't the only thing that's changed for the worse in the name of progress. He thinks women have changed too much, too.

"You don't find a man who rules his home nowadays. In my time, a woman stayed home. Nowadays she tells her husband, 'You aren't taking care of me—I have to have my own money.' She goes off somewhere to get some fine job.

"Old-timey women wasn't like the women we got now," Bruce says with a sigh. "To my thinking, women were more feminine then... they'd fall over—you know, faint—over just any little thing. That was mighty fine."

Though he doesn't cotton much to today's women, Bruce's life took on new meaning recently when Baylor's foster daughter and her baby, Michelle, moved to the farm. Bruce happily cleaned up and painted his old clapboard house and added a porch with a railing so the baby could play outside.

Bruce—who's outlived two wives—admits he'd marry again if he could find a woman with "old-timey" values. "But," he concedes, "it'd be hard for me to support her right on the two bits a day I make with my mules."

For now Bruce is fiercely proud of his "independent old age". Most days he's up at 5 a.m. and out with his mules.

"Work makes a man independent," he says flatly. "You learn about life through work and hard times, not through books. Kids today are weasely—they can't do nothin'.

"I don't know if there's any one thing that's made me live so long," Bruce adds with a twinkle in his eyes. "It could be that old Indian blood in me. But livin' right and cultivatin' yer life—that's what's important."

Bruce gets up to return to his mules—there's plenty more work for him and his team today. "You can build a life up or tear it down," he shouts over his shoulder. "Me, I take care of mine!"

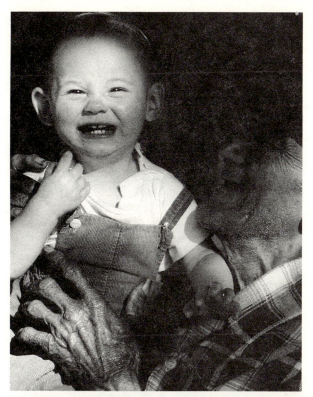

CONSTANT COMPANION "Jack" (above) is always near, and Bruce also enjoys visits with granddaughter (top) of brother Baylor (opposite page).

Dad's Solution Was 'Doin' and Eliminatin' '

By Robert Back

Back in 1948, times in Montgomery County, Kentucky weren't depressed—they were downright *caved-in*.

Back then, my family lived there on a 20-acre farm that was so scrubby it had trouble producing a good crop of healthy weeds. One year we made almost as much from the chewing tobacco advertisement on the side of our barn as we did from the corn crop.

Shucks, I was 10 years old before I learned that blackberry briars and rocks weren't our principal crops!

Although every new year seemed to be worse than the one before, each spring my eternally optimistic father declared *this* would be the year that put us over the top. A little hard work and a whole lot of faith in the almighty would be all it would take.

(I guess it never occurred to Dad that we'd been practicing those two virtues year in and year out, with no noticeable result to show for it...)

Dad was also a great one for encouraging us to keep our imaginations working right along with our hands and backs. He firmly believed every difficult job had at least two dozen easier ways of being done.

"Learn to do new things with what you have," he was fond of saying, "because doin' has a way of eliminatin' needin'."

And did we ever do! Every spring we'd pick rocks out of those fields by the thousands. We'd toss them onto our wagon, and Jake, our cantankerous mule, would pull load after load to the end of the field. Truth to tell, old Jake wasn't always thrilled about the job...and there were a few days when he frustrated the project by flatly refusing to pull the wagon 1 foot more.

But after we'd finally picked every rock bigger than a marble, the plowing would begin. My father would strip to the waist, hitch Jake to the plow and throw the check lines around his thick neck.

"All right, Jake," he'd say, "let's turn some ground."

From the first gray light of dawn until well after the sun had dropped behind the green hills in the west, my dad followed that mule and plow, turning layer after layer of moist, red clay over to meet the sun's warmth. Sweat poured down his chest and back, and blisters the size of half-dollars formed and quickly burst on the inside of both his thumbs.

None of that seemed to bother Dad, though. He'd keep right on exhorting Jake and guiding the plow as straight as a sharpshooter's aim.

But spring wasn't the only time of year in which we all kept busy. During the summer, my 12-year-old sister was assigned the job of taking care of the vegetable garden. As for my 14-year-old sister and me, the hot summer days found us scouring the creek banks and hillsides in search of blackberries and huckleberries.

After the day's supper dishes were washed and put away each summer night, my mother worked into the wee hours of the morning, making delicious jams and jellies. It was murderously hot over the wood-burning stove in our kitchen, and I can still hear my perspiring mother saying "Lord, have mercy!" over and over as she stirred the bubbling juices.

In the fall, after the corn was laid by, the winter's firewood cut and ranked and hickory logs cut for meat curing, we had more time on our hands. We filled those colorful late-autumn days by gathering walnuts, hickory nuts and hazelnuts. After they were hulled and dried in the sun for a few days, they were spread upon a piece of tin in the attic to await winter's snow.

Shortly after the first frost, we always butchered two hogs. While my mother and sisters rendered the lard and made lye soap in a galvanized washtub, my father and I cut up the meat.

Everything except the sides of bacon and the hams was salted down and put in the icehouse. The bacon and hams were hung from iron hooks in the smokehouse and washed down with mild salt water. Then a small fire was started, with hickory logs providing the fuel.

For the next 3 weeks or so, the meat was washed down every day with mild salt water, and the small fire was kept burning around the clock. At the end of that time, we'd have hickory-smoked ham, hot biscuits with wild honey, sweet potatoes and apple pie for supper. Nothing I've eaten since has tasted better.

Back in those days, it seemed our lives were forever governed by the processes of preparation. In the spring, preparations were made for the year's crops. In the summer, vegetables were canned and berries and fruits made into jams, preserves and jellies—all in preparation for the harsh winter ahead.

In the fall, the corn was harvested, firewood cut, hogs butchered and cured, and nuts gathered and squirreled away in the attic for use in those delicious, warm pastries that always tasted 10 times better when the snow was blowing outside. Finally, in the winter ice had to be cut and put in the icehouse for summer use.

Preparation. That word meant only one thing back then—a lot of back-breaking work! I now look back and realize that it meant much more.

It meant the structuring and strengthening of strong-willed characters. Initiative and self-sufficiency, the sturdy legs upon which character stands, became vital elements within our personalities.

They developed and grew with the steady and sure-fire consistency of those golden sunsets which marked the end of those weary days. Most of all, I came to appreciate my father's sage advice: "Learn to do new things with what you have," I can still hear him say, "because doin' has a way of eliminatin' needin'."

Amen to that, old-timer...and thanks, Dad, for being what you were.

Remember Days of Steam? They're Still Around Here!

By Barbara Clouser

Along with thousands of others every year, I bump across the fields of the Penns Cave Farm in our pickup, to the annual Nittany Antique Machinery Show held near Centre Hall, Pennsylvania.

There's an almost unexplainable charm about it. The setting is in the middle of Brush

Valley, one of Pennsylvania's prettiest farming areas.

But more important is the feeling—almost magical—of having stepped back in time to a rustic, more honest era. It's fascinating to watch chaff flying from an antique threshing machine...or to see the horse patiently walking round and round to power a gristmill.

My biggest problem at the show is deciding what to see first. Out in a field, farmers walk behind Belgians and Percherons. Harness buckles gleam under the warm fall sun and machinery clanks as the plows turn over the dark earth.

At noon each day, the shrill blasts of steam tractor whistles split the stillness of the valley. Puffs of black coal smoke darken the sky as the owners of the old tractors salute the crowd.

There are crafts of all kinds to try—you can put a few stitches in a quilt or watch a spinning wheel turn clumps of wool into yarn.

If you're hungry, you can sink your teeth into a real steak sandwich or enjoy a plateful of funnel cakes topped with powdered sugar.

The day wouldn't be complete without a stroll through the 4-acre antique flea market, where you can buy anything from tools to small collectibles.

As you wander through the crowd listening to folks, you slowly become aware that you're not only with Pennsylvanians but people from all across the country who enjoy seeing, smelling and listening to the sounds of yesteryear.

Seems as though everybody knows there's no better place to be than in the country...and no better trip to take than a trip back in time!

STEP BACK. *Farmers operating an old-time shingle mill (above) is just one of the delights for young and old alike at annual show. "You feel like you've stepped back to a more honest era," author says!*

He Climbed into the Saddle —And Never Came Down!

By Nita Wilson of Burden, Kansas

Oliver Darby is more than a cowboy. Still active and spry at 84, Oliver is a cowboy living legend. He's been riding horses so long he can't remember the first time he was on one. And he's been breaking horses for an incredible 77 years!

Today, Oliver still puts in a 5-day workweek. His home, Moline, is in the Kansas Flint Hills—grassland country—so he still helps area ranchers at roundup time. Tuesdays, Thursdays and Fridays are spent driving stock at three different livestock auctions.

Oliver keeps so busy, in fact, that he needs *two* horses. "That way," he explains, "I don't work one too long. They need their rest, too, you know."

John Brazle, owner of the Winfield Livestock Auction, one of the three Oliver regularly works, has nothing but praise for the legendary cowboy.

"Oliver may be 84 years old," John says

in awe, "but he's one of the best hands I've ever had. He's very loyal and he never misses a day of work.

"That's not all—his personality is tops. I'll tell you this—if everybody was like Oliver, this would be a whole lot better world!"

Oliver was born near Gentry, Missouri, but when he was 2 his parents moved to Hennessey, Oklahoma, where Oliver's dad found work breaking horses and serving as a ranch hand.

It was just a few years after that that Oliver had the first experience he can remember with a horse...and quite an experience it was!

Oliver was only 5, but his father took him on a weeklong trail ride across Oklahoma. "I had my own little bay horse," Oliver proudly remembers. "He was a one-eyed horse named Nick, but he was a dandy!"

Not long after that, when Oliver was 7, the family moved back to Missouri, where his father worked on a dairy for a man named Pruitt.

"Mr. Pruitt had given his son a spoiled Shetland pony that kept bucking the boy off," Oliver recalls. "I'd never broken a horse before, but I told my father I'd sure like to try with that pony. I've been breaking horses ever since."

Oliver's broken so many horses over the past 77 years that he's lost track of the number. Some he remembers as being difficult and wild, and he recollects a number of "close calls". Yet, the most serious injury he's ever suffered breaking a horse is a sprained wrist.

Oliver's had some amazing experiences—back when he was 44, Oliver broke 75 head of horses at one time.

Here's how that happened: A big ranch in New Mexico had been turned over to the Boy Scouts, and the cattle and horses were being sold. A rancher Oliver worked for at the time, along with another rancher, bought 105 head of the horses. Among the 105 head were 75 horses 3 and 4 years old who'd been branded but never broken.

The two ranchers promptly turned those horses over to Oliver to break, and he worked all summer on that single project. Sure enough, when the annual horse sale came around that November, Oliver had all 75 head ready to show.

Oliver says he's been making his own way in the world ever since he broke his first horse, and he's been involved in every aspect of ranch life during his many years as a cowboy.

One job he especially remembers began when he was 14 and lasted 2 years. He hired out to a man named Orv Carter, who had 700 to 800 longhorns near Woodward, Oklahoma.

At that time the country around Woodward was virtually unsettled, and a man could ride for miles and never see a fence. Oliver herded cattle on an isolated piece of land.

After sunup each day, Oliver turned the cattle out to graze. Then, about noon, he'd turn them to begin grazing back toward the pen where they'd spend the night. When Oliver needed to replenish his own food supply he'd

NO GRASS GROWS under Oliver Darby's feet—a lifelong cowboy, he's still going strong at age 84, regularly driving cattle at livestock auctions. He keeps so busy that he needs two horses..."That way, I don't work one too long," he says. "They need their rest, too!"

ride to a small trading post a number of miles away.

"I got $20 a month for that job—pretty good money back then for a young cowboy like me," Oliver recalls warmly. "But I finally quit because it was too lonely."

Oliver has little formal education. But much of the knowledge he's acquired isn't found in any books.

"My father always told me, 'Don't watch someone that has a good horse, a good saddle and a good outfit. You watch somebody that knows what he's doing,'" Oliver observes.

"I never forgot that piece of advice...and, you know, sometimes I've seen boys that had the poorest outfits that were sure the best cowhands."

At 84, Oliver says he feels fortunate to still have his good health.

"I never got rich," Oliver notes, "but I've sure enjoyed my work. I worked for two ranchers that told me I'd made them a million dollars. Back when I learned this business, you had to run a ranch as cheap as you could, as good as you could, if you wanted to hold your job."

Oliver permits himself a smile of satisfaction. "If I had to live my life over, I'd want to live it the same way. The Lord's been good to me."

"I NEVER GOT RICH," Oliver says of his life as a cowboy. *"But looking back I wouldn't change a thing."*

Getting Clipped at Jim's Is Still a Shear Bargain

By Mack Barrett of La Vergne, Tennessee

The 5¢ cup of coffee and the nickel cigar may be only fond memories...but the 25¢ haircut is alive and kicking at Jim Borren's barbershop in Woodbury, Tennessee.

A *quarter cut*, in a day when many barbers charge $10 or more? It's true! But it's not just the price that keeps the rural residents of Woodbury coming back to Jim's.

Jim's shop is in an antiquated blue building, which sports a faded advertisement for an old-time soft drink. Inside the shop looks more like an early-20th century "tonsorial parlor" than a 1980's barbershop (you can almost *hear* the old jingle "Shave and a haircut, two bits" when you walk in!).

A potbellied stove sits in the middle of the floor to provide warmth on chilly days, and a bare light bulb supported by a dangling drop cord supplies all the light Jim needs to do his job.

Then there's Jim's barber chair. "It's older than I am, that's for sure," chuckles Jim...and Jim is 84 years old!

Jim hasn't always cut hair—he worked a small farm before taking up barbering in the mid-1940's. "I cut my brother's hair one day," he recalls, "and everyone liked it real well...so I decided that's what I wanted to do."

When Jim opened his shop, he charged 25¢ for a haircut—and he's never raised that price. How does he do it?

"It's simple," Jim quips, with a twinkle in his eye. "I cut a customer's hair...and he gives me 25¢!"

Then, turning serious for a moment, he explains: "Well, I'll tell you—I don't have a car, don't have a television, don't have a lot of expenses that other people have.

"I don't try to live high on the hog. I'm still living in the good old days...and that's what I like. Seems people were happier then; they didn't have so much to worry about."

Jim lives in the back of his small shop. "That makes it real handy," he says with a smile. "When it's raining or snowing outside, I don't have to get out in it to come to work."

Business now isn't quite as brisk as when Jim was one of the few barbers in town and men wore their hair shorter—"I've had both benches here full and people standing up waiting for haircuts," he remembers. But Jim still keeps plenty busy.

His shop is open 6 days a week, 7 a.m. until 5 p.m.—like his price, those hours have never changed. Jim allows 15 minutes per haircut and says he averages 20 heads a day.

Jim gives only the basic, bowl-style haircut. "I never did try to learn this modern hairstyling business," he says with a wave of his hand. "Back when everybody got simple hair-

CUT-RATE PRICE is what Jim Borren offers every day— but it's not just the 25¢ haircut that keeps his barber chair full. Jim's customers appreciate the unhurried, old-time feeling the barbershop exudes. "I don't live high on the hog," Jim says. "I'm still in the good old days."

cuts, before they all let their hair grow long, there wasn't enough *time* to spend an hour on one head—so I just never started doing it."

If you're in the market for a fancy hairstyle, Jim Borren's barbershop is probably the last place you should visit.

But if you'd like a good, honest haircut and a trip back into the unhurried days of the past—rolled together into a 25¢ bargain—well, just step up into the chair...Jim's always ready to clip and chat.

'Stubborn Dutchman' Takes Tractor Over Wheelchair!

By Steve Begnoche of Morenci, Michigan

There's an old saying that if a person wants something enough, he'll walk through fire to get it. Glenn Rupp knows all about that.

In 1980, after farming for nearly half a century, Glenn was partially paralyzed by a cyst on his spinal column and lost the use of both legs. For most folks, that would have ended an active life and marked the beginning of life in a wheelchair. But Glenn had other ideas. So with the blessing of his doctors at the Mayo Clinic in Minnesota, the loving support of his wife, family and friends, and a hefty dose of determination, Glenn found some ingenious ways to keep right on farming.

"Farming is something I knew I could do," says Glenn. "Plowing my fields is a lot easier than just sitting in a wheelchair all the time."

Glenn has farmed for 51 of his 61 years— 30 of them at his 161-acre place near Wauseon, Ohio. He's also worked as a plumbing and heating contractor.

"Originally, I started the plumbing business just to supplement the farm income," Glenn explains. "Unfortunately, sometimes the tail seemed to be wagging the dog!"

Glenn never ceased trying to put the "tail" back in place, however. "It was always my intention to retire to the farm," he states. "I just didn't expect to be handicapped when I reached that point."

Yet *because* of his handicap, farming has taken on a new meaning for Glenn. "It gives me a real psychological lift," he says. "I have the satisfaction of accomplishing something each day, and it tends to distract me from the frustration of my handicap."

Obviously, much had to be accomplished before Glenn could drive a tractor into the field again. Three tractors and a farm truck had to be

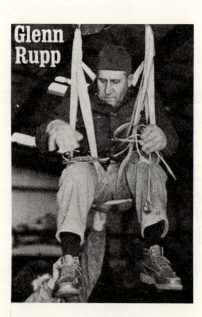

FIGHTING FARMER Glenn Rupp can't walk to his fields, but he won't let paralysis keep him off his tractor.

modified to meet Glenn's special needs.

"One of the most difficult problems," Glenn explains, "was designing the necessary hand controls for the different tractors. After several weeks of experimenting, we finally decided on rigid extensions of the original pedals. It was the simplest way to go, and it proved to be the most satisfactory."

The new controls are easy for Glenn to reach and also provide him with a needed grip—without using his legs to steady himself, Glenn must have hold of something at all times or he'll tumble off the tractor.

Just getting on and off the tractor was a problem that had to be solved mechanically, with the design and construction of a special hoist. With help from his wife, Pat, Glenn now straps a harness around himself and is raised onto the tractor seat. Not too dignified, Glenn admits...but it sure works.

Glenn also faces unique problems once he gets to his fields. "I have to be extra cautious to avoid wet holes, tight corners or anything that would normally require using my legs," Glenn reveals. If he does get stuck, Glenn must alert Pat or a passerby—and that's not always easy.

"Once I was out in the field while Pat was in town getting seed beans," Glenn remembers. "On the first round I attempted, I got stuck within about 100 feet of the road.

"I shouted for the nearest neighbors, but they weren't home. Finally, I managed to alert the lady who carries our mail. She got help from a more distant neighbor."

Glenn chuckles. "I was stuck out there getting a good suntan for 45 minutes!"

It's not unusual for Glenn to laugh like that at the problems his handicap has presented. He admits, however, that the paralysis is often frustrating.

"But there are ways of coping with that," he quickly adds. "My faith in God helps me accept the inevitable—when I'm in a situation I can't control, I often turn to prayer."

Glenn doesn't accept his paralysis as inevitable, however. And, someday, he may even be able to get up on the tractor by himself again. For with the help of leg braces and crutches, and skilled physical therapists who are as determined as he to see him back on his feet, Glenn is learning to walk again.

Glenn quickly points out he hasn't made the progress he has all by himself. "I'm not only willing to accept suggestions, I'm also willing to accept help whenever I can get it," he says. "Sometimes it's just impossible to get a job done without help. I'm especially grateful for my good neighbors."

Glenn also credits Pat, who's always been a full-time partner on the farm. Sometimes, however, Glenn admits he must do a good job of convincing her that farming is what he should be doing.

"One of the big problems in returning to farming was Pat's reluctance to accept the idea it could be beneficial for me," says Glenn. "I'm sure she was afraid that I might get injured in the process."

Pat nods and says she still worries when it's time to harvest their 50 acres of soybeans and 50 acres of alfalfa.

"If I don't hear the tractor when I should, I go out and look, or I call the neighbors at the nearest place to where he should be and ask if they've seen him," says Pat. "I hear or see him about every half hour, but I try not to get uptight about it. I do my garden work or whatever."

For Pat, "whatever" can include changing

oil in a tractor, truck or car, attaching implements, buying seed and fertilizer, selling grain and doing the 1,001 jobs that need doing to keep a farm and home going.

"I enjoy living on the farm, and, when I have time, I even enjoy getting out in the fields in the spring," she reveals.

"Since Glenn became paralyzed," Pat continues, "we're apt to go about the work a little differently, but we still get it done."

Glenn agrees. "Because of my situation, I've sort of turned the entire farm operation over to my wife." With a twinkle in his eye, he adds, "I simply serve as *her* assistant now!"

Pat smiles. "I think Glenn wants to farm too many acres—he wants to plant 40 more this year!"

But Glenn is ready with plenty of reasons why farming more acres is practical, even for a farmer who's paralyzed. Pat just listens; she knows he won't give in once his mind is made up.

And so, Glenn continues hoisting himself aboard his tractor and heading out to do what he's always done. Farmers are a determined lot, and Glenn's certainly no different...farming often means overcoming obstacles or hardships, even for farmers who *can* walk.

"I guess I've just always been a stubborn Dutchman," Glenn chuckles.

And a farmer, too—that says it all.

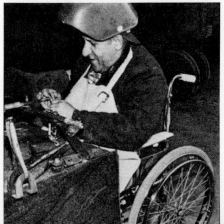

NOT ALONE in his determination to continue farming, Glenn relies heavily on wife Pat (top left) for moral support and assistance and modifies tractor controls to operate by hand.

27

Farm Couple's Teamwork Brings Past Back to Life

By Pat Gibes of Port Washington, Wisconsin

On one of those lyrical late-summer days, the cicadas fill the air with song and the dust lies heavy along the country roadside. It's a golden, glorious day of ripening grain, red-winged blackbirds and day lilies gone wild.

Across the road, Albert and Lucille Sudbrink are beginning to harvest, turning their field into a crazy quilt of oats—standing, bundled, arranged in shocks.

The pair works in harmony, Albert skillfully eyeballing the old tractor along straight rows while Lucille rides on the strange-looking paddle-wheeled contraption he pulls.

"There are always people who stop to watch us," Albert comments proudly. The curious soon learn the couple is cutting and binding oats with an antique binder—purchased 30 years ago for $25.

Even in conversation, explaining how they do their shocking, Albert and Lucille function as a harmonious unit.

"You set the bundles north and south—" Albert begins.

"—so the wind dries them—" Lucille continues.

"—about 10 to a shock—"

"—with the heads to the inside."

Then, once the grain is dried, the bundles are loaded by hand onto the wagon and are ready for threshing.

"My dad is 93 years old," Albert says, "and he still comes every year to see me threshing. In his day, Dad was famous for his threshing rig."

That reputation is sure to stay in the Sudbrink family, since Albert's thresher is quite a showstopper itself. Like the binder, the threshing machine is an antique, purchased at auction for $95.

In fact, *all* the machinery the Sudbrinks use is antique. They work a 20-acre farm just south of Port Washington, Wisconsin, near the Lake Michigan shoreline.

IN WITH THE OLD. Albert and Lucille Sudbrink do every bit of the work on their Wisconsin farm with antique machinery. "It's not a money-making proposition," Albert admits. "But you can't retire and do nothing."

PITCHING IN TOGETHER, Albert and Lucille work in perfect harmony to complete their harvest. In a typical year, the Sudbrinks harvest 500 bushels of oats, 200 bales of straw, 800 bales of hay—and lots of memories.

Albert is 63 years old and a retired machinist. But all his life he's been farming, before and after regular working hours. At age 60, Lucille has spent her entire life farming.

The Sudbrink farm shows the result of years under their tender, loving stewardship.

Now that the Sudbrinks' three daughters have grown and moved away, the farm is much smaller than in past years. But Albert and Lucille are able to provide for most all their needs from the farm.

They have a large vegetable garden and they raise hay, oats and corn for the animals and some wheat for the chickens. Their farm has a few cows providing milk, plus chickens for eggs and the table, and feeder pigs for market.

While the Sudbrinks don't farm on a large scale, they do work mostly by hand, using traditional methods. And the hard work—which they've always shared—brings them pleasure.

"There's nothing on the farm we don't do together," Lucille says. "I know his ways, and he knows mine."

"Farming the old way is a dying art," Albert says sadly, as Lucille nods her agreement.

"Understand, we don't recommend doing it our way to anyone starting out," Albert is quick to point out. "It certainly isn't a money-making proposition. But we're not rushed—we can do what we want whenever we feel like doing it."

"It's a very simple life," Lucille says softly.

"Some people may think we're foolish," Albert adds, "but you can't retire and do nothing."

"It's the *best* kind of life for us," Lucille concludes.

Albert and Lucille gaze at each other across the kitchen table—and, as if by now they can read each other's thoughts, they smile in unison.

"We've had *good* years, Ma!" Albert exclaims.

And both smiles grow brighter.

Grandson Knew Best Bait...

A FARMER who's also a grandpa shares this humorous, heartwarming tale:

"One Sunday morning our minister chose fishing as the topic of his 'children's chat' before the services," says James White of Ellendale, North Dakota.

"With all the little youngsters gathered around him in front of the congregation, the minister asked, 'When you go fishing, what do you take along to catch fish?'

"Several children piped up with suggestions of bait or a boat or fishing rods...but my little grandson shouted loud enough to be heard over 'em all: 'I take *Grandpa!*' "

'Old Man' Teaches Kids Shining Secrets of Cattle

By Frank Yoder of Kalona, Iowa

Seasoned cattlemen recognize Russ Brannen as one of the top beef-grooming experts in the Midwest, and the dozens of trophies on display at his Muscatine, Iowa home back up their opinion.

Still, more than the respect of his fellow cattlemen, more than the prizes he's won, the 72-year-old rancher treasures most the compliment paid him when someone said, "Every kid needs an old man like Russ."

More than 30 years ago, Russ started teaching cattle fitting and grooming to 4-H and FFA youngsters. Two generations and thousands of kids later, he's still going strong.

Russ' cattle-grooming expertise goes back a long way. "I was a farm manager in South Dakota in the 1930's," he says. "I worked for an old fellow there, and he and I used to mix our own oils and stuff to put on the cattle before we took them to a sale.

"Even if we were just sellin' them out private, we always dressed 'em up a bit. That's where I learned a good-looking animal always sells higher than a plain looker."

Russ put those cattle beauty secrets to good use many years later after he'd moved to Iowa and was working for Kent Feeds.

"When I started runnin' the feed routes, I realized that few kids had dads who'd been in 4-H themselves. The dads didn't know how to help their kids with their projects," he says.

"I was always giving advice to kids on my route about grooming and showing their cattle, and before long it sorta turned into a class where several kids could learn at once."

When Russ started the classes, he figured they'd last maybe 3 years. Now, it's been 33 years, and the classes have spread to 10 states. "It just kept growing and growing," Russ says with a shake of his head.

Russ isn't one who believes judges look only at the animal and not at how carefully it's been groomed.

"Fittin' cattle for show is just like a lady goin' to the beauty parlor and gettin' all fixed up, and then wearin' the right clothes to go with it," he says.

"You know," he adds with a friendly grin, "if you pass a plain Jane walkin' down the street, you're not very apt to take any notice of her. But if you meet a classy lady, it's almost automatic to take a second look. It's the same way with a cattle judge."

As for grooming techniques, Russ tells the kids to grab the bull by its horns. "All it takes to run a pair of clippers is guts and go-ahead," he says. "Most kids have guts, but when they get those clippers in their hand, their go-ahead kinda disappears.

"FITTIN' CATTLE for show is just like a lady going to the beauty parlor," Russ says. "The judges notice."

"They're afraid they'll do something wrong," Russ continues. "I always tell 'em to use the neighbor kid's calf to practice on!" he adds with a laugh.

Russ and Dorothy have been married 48 years. They live on a small ranch overlooking the Mississippi River, where Russ raises Black Angus cattle.

Their place got its name—"Eight Ball Acres"—back when their son was in 4-H. "The first steer our son ever won a show with he named 'Little Eight Ball' after a cartoon character," Russ explains. "When we got to registerin' our Angus cows, we registered them as Eight Ball Acres Angus, and the name's stuck."

Russ grew up in the now-vanished small town of Baird, Kansas. "My mother was a widow who took in sewin' to feed us kids," he recalls. "There were times when we'd buy a hog heart for a dime because we could slice that up and get three meals from it."

The family also lived in Iowa and South Dakota, and Russ moved back to Iowa for good in 1933. As a young man in Iowa, he did a variety of farm jobs, from milking cows and replacing wheels on windmills to traveling with a hay baling crew.

Russ knows each of his 28 cows by name and by character. He can tell you every detail about them—down to how many show winners the black cow over by the creek has calved, and

ON THE BALL. Ranch's first show winner was named for old-time cartoon character. Russ registered his cows as "Eight Ball Acres Angus"—and the name stuck!

where they all are today.

Come next summer, Russ will be back on the road, again helping kids with their animals. "I like kids, and I enjoy having them around," he says. "They keep me young."

At the rate Russ is going, he's one "old man" who'll never grow old.

50th Wedding Anniversary Really Got Farmer Rolling

By Ed Klimuska of Ronks, Pennsylvania

The whole town was abuzz. The biggest event in Bowmansville, Pennsylvania in a long time was about to occur, and word had gotten around

There, at the head of Main Street, stood retired farmer Frank Hersh, all decked out in his "Sunday finest". A determined look was on his face as he gripped the handles of an old-fashioned wooden wheelbarrow.

Frank's wife of 50 years, Irene, was there, too...in fact, you might say she'd come along for the ride. The time had finally arrived for Frank to "get moving" on a 25-year-old promise.

What in the world was going on here? Well, you see, 25 years earlier, on their 25th wedding anniversary, Frank had told Irene: "If we're still married 25 years from now, I'll push you through Bowmansville in a wheelbarrow!" Exactly 25 years later, Frank and Irene were

31

finally ready to begin rolling for real!

He may not have been entirely serious when he made his unusual promise, but Frank was serious now...and a hush fell over the

WHERE THERE'S A WHEEL...there's a way, farmer Frank Hersh proved. He was as good as his word when push came to love and he fulfilled vow he'd made to his wife, Irene.

crowd lining Main Street as Irene eased herself into the wheelbarrow, newly painted in bright red for the occasion.

Frank, 68, had chosen a downhill route, explaining, "I didn't tell her which *way* I'd push her through town!" Still, the 8 blocks looming ahead seemed more like 8 miles to Frank.

Frank chewed gum to ease the tension. When someone in the crowd yelled, "Are you going to make it, Paw?" Frank nodded with a determined smile. "I said I would, and I will!" he shouted.

And he did. Amid the cheers of nearly 300 well-wishers, a huffing, puffing Frank pushed a smiling, waving Irene 8 blocks through Bowmansville to the village's park pavilion, where a picnic with family and friends awaited.

Irene was all set to join the celebration at the end of her ride, but Frank was still a little winded. "Near the end there, it was really pulling on my muscles," he admitted. "I had trouble balancing her, too, because she was waving so much to the crowd. But I made it!"

Among the guests at the picnic were Frank and Irene's eight children, 20 grandchildren and four great-grandchildren. Frank and Irene still live on their 78-acre farm, and Frank got in shape for his historic push by chopping and hauling loads of firewood.

What will Frank do for an encore? Well, he's already made Irene another promise. "For our 75th anniversary," he says, "I promised to buy us a love seat."

One with *rollers*, Frank?

Nebraska Brothers Enjoy Well-Rounded Retirement

By B. Paul Chicoine of Sioux City, Iowa

Happiness, to Fred and Donald Lembke, is the jangle of a four-horse hitch and the sway of a high-wheeled wagon.

That's why, after nearly 50 years of farming together, the Newcastle, Nebraska brothers have turned their 1,000-acre farm over to a

nephew's care.

Now they're busy keeping 'em rolling... wagons and wooden wheels, that is.

The Lembke brothers have become so renowned in their new hobby that Harnessmaker Acres (their 80-acre farm and work site) has grown into a mecca for old farmwagon and implement buffs from far and wide in need of wheels and repairs.

The Lembkes' specialty is building and rebuilding old wooden wheels. "Other than some fellow down in Lincoln who builds wagons for museums, I guess we're the only darn fools doing this kind of work anymore," Donald says with a laugh.

This retirement hobby is no small undertaking by these Nebraska brothers. Since turning full-time to the almost-forgotten trade, they've accumulated three full workshops bulging with tools and supplies...and a farm full of "patients".

The hillsides above their wheel and wagon shops are filled with rows of wagons, mowers, planters, rakes, cultivators and other horse-drawn farm equipment awaiting restoration. Other clearings contain piles of deteriorating farm and dray wagons the brothers have gleaned from fence rows and auctions throughout northern and eastern Nebraska.

Those relics, together with stacks of curing oak, hickory and other home-grown and home-sawn woods from the brothers' small farm, provide the raw materials for the pair's labors.

Wheels are restored in a special shop on one of two "wheel tables" constructed by Fred and Don themselves. Power tools adapted from ancient "pointers" and "dowelers" are used in fitting the components together.

The brothers say building a wagon wheel takes a day or so.

"We don't push it," Don explains. "We're just a couple of old bachelors, having fun with what we're doing and doing it at our own pace."

Brother Fred nods. "If we pushed it," he smiles, "it wouldn't be fun anymore, would it?"

WOODEN WONDERS. Rare dray wagon at right is just one of the many restoration jobs the Lembke brothers have taken on. "We're just a couple old bachelors having fun at our own pace," Don explains.

ROLLING ON! Donald (at left in photo above) and Fred keep busy in retirement restoring wagon wheels.

Here Comes the Judge!

BUYING OR SELLING a horse in West Virginia can be risky business.

Like many states, West Virginia still has some odd laws on its books—holdovers from the "good old days".

In West Virginia, you're breaking the law if you buy or sell a horse within a mile of a church, religious camp meeting or fair. It's also illegal to wear a hat in a theater or opera house.

The horse transaction could earn you a $50 fine, under an 1899 law. Wearing a hat in a theater, says an 1897 law, could cost you a fine of $2 to $10 (probably depends on hat size).

A current state legislator has introduced a bill to repeal these two laws. Maybe he's got a horse to sell...

33

He Pounds Out a Living As a Country Tinsmith

By John Danicic of Mumford, New York

He calls it "poor-man's silver". "To some folks," says tinsmith Ralph Rubenstein, "the word tin means cheap or second-class. But there was a time not so long ago when tin was very valuable to rural families."

Farm families used to drink from tin cups and dine on tin plates. On dark mornings and evenings they used windproof tin lanterns to light the barn while milking into sturdy tin pails.

"Tin was once the most common material for everything from plates to furniture," Ralph asserts.

Before he says more, Ralph points out that what he's really talking about is tin-plated steel or iron. "Pure tin is too soft to hold a shape," he explains. "Early tin-plate was made by dipping sheets of iron over and over into a vat of melted tin."

The resulting pliable metal sheets were formed into cookie cutters, coffeepots, shaving mugs and washboards.

According to Ralph, the tin peddler was America's first traveling salesman. "He'd rattle into town aboard his wagonload of tin goods two or three times a year, and rural folks would swap food or produce to get the tin items they needed."

It's obvious Ralph knows plenty about tin …and it's a knowledge he loves to share with others. He even remembers the very first item

TINNIN' 'N' TALKIN'. Museum visitors watch and listen with interest as Ralph creates useful and decorative items from tin…all the while expounding on the history of tinsmithing in America. Above: finished items.

he ever made from tin, long, long ago.

"I was 9 years old," he recounts. "My dad farmed with horses near Macedon, New York, and whenever I wasn't helping with chores, I was building things.

"One day I saw a picture in an old magazine of a 'tin-can sailboat'," he goes on. "I made one and had hours of fun sailing it around in the horse trough!"

His skills with metal served Ralph well with farm repairs, and later in a career as a millwright and mechanic. But it wasn't until retirement that he once more began casting a crafty eye at tin cans.

"I was at one of those 'living-history' museums," Ralph says, "watching a craftsman making a punched tin lantern, and I got to thinking about all the tin cans I had at home."

Ralph went home to his shop and cut up an empty 5-gal. salad oil can to fashion his own lantern.

"I can't even count how many I've made since," he adds.

Ralph constructed many more items from tin, and word of his skills began to spread. Friends and neighbors bought pieces, and before long, collectors and decorators were ordering lanterns and candleholders.

When the Genesee County Outdoor Museum opened in 1977, Ralph heard that there was an authentic early-American tin shop in need of a smith. He was the first (and only) person in line to apply for the job. "There aren't a

OLD AND NEW. An electric soldering iron is the only concession Ralph makes to modern times in his work.

lot of tinsmiths around looking for work," he admits.

Now, for 6 days a week from May to October each year, Ralph does the two things he loves most—working with tin and talking about tin.

Tinsmithing won't be a forgotten art as long as Ralph has his way…he's still doing the best he can!

This 91-Year-Old Pilot Makes a Dandy Duster

By Willard and Elma Waltner

He's a pioneer. No…Clyde Ice didn't arrive in South Dakota in a covered wagon. But he did pioneer a practice that revolutionized farming—Clyde claims to be the first person ever to spray farmland from an airplane.

"I was running a flying service in the Black Hills back in 1937," Clyde recalls. "The sugar beet farmers there were having webworm problems and asked me if I could apply insecticide powder from my plane. I told 'em I'd give it a try!"

Clyde wired an eaves spout along the fuselage of his tiny Piper Cub, with an elbow joint leading into the backseat.

"I flew over the beet fields just high enough to keep from touching the leaves while my partner poured the insecticide through a funnel into the spout.

"It was a crude way of doing it," Clyde admits, "but we sure got rid of those worms!"

Over the following years, Clyde sprayed anything that needed spraying...more beets, corn, wheat, even towns (for flies and mosquitoes).

Gradually he modified his plane to carry a liquid tank and sprayers, and eventually had a larger plane built especially for spraying.

Clyde still flies today, but he leaves most of the spraying to his son, Cecil.

"I could still be spraying," Clyde asserts, "but my knees bother me and my feet go to sleep. My plane has foot brakes, and when I need brakes, I can't afford to wait for my feet to wake up!

"Besides," Clyde continues, "I'm tired of gettin' up at 3 a.m. to get some spraying done before the wind picks up."

Clyde has covered plenty of air in his years of flying. In addition to spraying, he's carried mail, herded wild horses, hunted coyotes and searched for uranium. During World War II, Clyde gave flight training to 2,000 young Air Force cadets.

Pretty good for a pilot who never had a flying lesson in his life!

FLYING HIGH. Old photo above shows Clyde in early days as a rural "barnstormer". Clyde still flies today but now leaves the spraying to his son, Cecil.

Taking a Bite Out of Crime!

"MY 3-YEAR-OLD NIECE, Staci, had been staying with Grandma while Grandpa was out of town," Carol Ann Oard of Colby, Kansas writes.

"By the time Grandpa returned from his trip, Staci had grown accustomed to seeing Grandma remove her dentures for cleaning—and she just happened to walk into the bathroom as Grandpa was popping his own dentures into his mouth.

"Staci took in that scene, and her eyes grew wide. She dashed from the bathroom, shouting, 'Grandma—Grandpa has *your* teeth!' "

The Good Old Days?

THE FARMER'S 11-year-old grandson sat slumped in front of the TV set with a bored expression. Finally, his grandfather could stand it no longer and said: "When I was your age, I walked miles through blizzards, milked seven cows before breakfast every morning and rode a horse to school instead of taking a comfortable bus. What do you think of that?"

The boy looked up and said, "Gee, Grandpa, I wish we could have fun like that."

FOND MEMORIES. Clyde's most cherished memento is photo of Ford Tri-Motor, America's first airliner.

Oregon Cattleman Likes To Just Fiddle Around!

By Virgil Rupp of Pendleton, Oregon

His hobby might seem a bit unusual for a rugged rancher, so Oregon cattleman Ralph Low usually keeps quiet about it. But he doesn't have to say much...the beautiful violins he painstakingly crafts by hand speak for themselves—in perfect musical tones.

Ralph's violins have won national awards for workmanship and tone quality, but his only tools are a sharp knife, a coping saw and some scrapers. A rancher all his life, Ralph began making violins just 7 years ago, when a back injury forced him to take it easy for a while on his Bear Creek ranch in eastern Oregon's Umatilla County.

"My grandfather used to make violins," Ralph explains, "so I guess I sort of inherited the talent. I work very slowly, spending up to 500 hours on each violin to make sure it's *just* right. Sometimes I've turned out three or four violins a year...sometimes only one."

Ralph says he's turned over most of the chores on his "10,000 acres of rocks" to his son Wayne and son-in-law Allen. The ranch has about 500 acres of wheat, and the rest is pasture for a commercial beef herd of Herefords, Simmentals, Limousins and Chianinas.

"When my back's not hurting," Ralph chuckles, "I prefer being outside doing ranch work. So the number of violins I make depends a lot on how my back feels!"

Ralph uses no power tools to cut and shape the maple and spruce into instruments that look as lovely as they sound. "Power tools go too fast," he says. "It's too easy to make mistakes." Instead, Ralph uses a wide variety of scrapers—some are made of glass—to shape the spruce tops and maple bottoms of the violins to the thicknesses needed to produce the proper tone.

In addition to making violins, Ralph also repairs them, and he's much in demand among musicians all over the Pacific Northwest—from country fiddlers to concert violinists!

Ralph only shakes his head when some folks compare his work with that of master violin maker Antonius Stradivarius. But who knows...someday one of Ralph's handmade violins just might be as famous. After all, there aren't many violin makers who've gone from "herd" to "heard"!

SLOW TO BOW. Using hand tools, Ralph crafts violins from spruce and maple. Resulting tones are a delight!

'Molly' and 'Dolly' Help Farmer Take His Pick

By Murray Lee

"Giddup Molly, Dolly," Ed Mason calls to the Belgian draft horses. The mares plod up the corn row on Ed's farm near Marshalltown, Iowa until he stops them with a "Whoaa!"

The team creaks to a halt, and Ed jumps out of the wagon and starts picking corn ear by ear, working quickly as a crisp wind rustles the cornhusks. The horses don't seem to mind the chilly weather. They placidly stand in their harness awaiting the next command. Molly's the mare next to the corn, and she occasionally snitches an ear when Ed turns his back.

Ed usually harvests his corn with a tractor and picker. But last fall he left a few rows standing to handpick, just for the experience. "I've never done it this way before, and I thought I'd give it a try," Ed says. "I grew up with horses as a kid, and I always wanted to work with them."

Ed borrowed Molly and Dolly from a neighbor and harnessed them to an old steel-wheel wagon rigged with a sideboard to stop the corn as it's pitched in. When Ed heads for the field, he clambers into the back of the wagon. His dog, Teddy, hops in for the ride, too.

Those big, beautiful Belgians may not be as fast as a tractor, Ed notes, but it's satisfying to feel their gentle strength as they pull the wagon. They don't seem to be straining themselves. "They haven't even worked up a sweat," Ed says with a grin. "Guess I'll have to think of somethin' else for 'em to do."

BACK TO BASICS. Iowa farmer Ed Mason usually harvests his corn with the most up-to-date equipment. But he recently decided to relive his youth and handpick a few rows by borrowing a neighbor's Belgian draft horses.

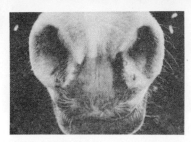

'Pride of Grandpa' Keep This Farmer's Hands Full

After he retired from farming, Clarence Strater got busy—in the kitchen, that is—and joined the ranks of "Men Who Run the Range". He'd always had an interest in baking, but his farming tasks just didn't allow time for culinary efforts.

His three grown daughters—Louise, Mary Ann and Marcia—had participated in the 4-H Foods Projects some 30 years ago, and Clarence remembers being interested at that time in what they were making, whether they'd opened a box or made it from scratch. "I was always willing to eat the results of their efforts," he says, "including their 'flops'."

When he retired from his Fort Wayne,

HE'S COOKING! Clarence Strater got late start in the kitchen—but he's making up for lost time now!

Indiana farm at age 68, some 13 years ago, Clarence finally found the time to "putz around" in the kitchen. He began with cookies and did a good enough job that they became instant favorites with his family and friends.

Soon he served those tasty morsels to members of his wife Lucile's two Home Extension clubs, NEO and at family holiday gatherings. He also presented them as gifts.

His cookies became such favorites that Clarence's daughters and his seven grandchildren tried to persuade him to enter the Senior Citizens' Cookie Bake-Off at the Indiana State Fair.

"I didn't think I was ready for oven-to-oven competition," Clarence admits. "But the kids wouldn't take no for an answer. That year, my Christmas presents included measuring cups and an apron!"

Then Clarence's married daughter, Marcia Partridge—who lives in Indianapolis, site of the State Fair—got all the information on the bake-off and entered her dad.

After a bit of "foot-dragging", Clarence finally gave in and consented to bake cookies for the contest. When fair time arrived, he pre-measured the ingredients, packed them along with his equipment and traveled the 110 miles to "Indy".

Every family member that could do so made the trip to the fair to root Clarence to victory. Their enthusiasm was rewarded—Clarence's cookies won the blue ribbon!

Clarence named his prize-winning cookies "Pride of Iowa". However, Clarence's family nicknamed them "Pride of Grandpa".

After 4 years, Clarence felt ready to move on to other things. One granddaughter, Lu Ann Schoenemann, had just completed a project in 4-H, and another granddaughter, Susan Bredemeyer, was about to get baking with her 4-H yeast rolls, so Clarence decided to try his hand at yeast rolls.

"Susan and I both baked up a batch of rolls on the same day, then compared the results," he says. It seemed to family taste-testers that Clarence's rolls were just a smidgen better.

About this same time, the Allen County 4-H Fair announced an open competition for cooks, and one of the classes happened to be yeast rolls. Granddaughter Lu Ann said, "Grandpa, if you bake the rolls, I'll take them to the fair."

Clarence was reluctant to enter another cooking contest, but once again the family prevailed. A batch of buttermilk pecan yeast rolls was baked, delivered to the fair and judged. The result? Blue ribbon Number Two!

In addition to his award-winning baking, Clarence plants and cares for a large garden each year. While he's supposedly retired from farming, he helps his son-in-law, Paul Schoenemann, plant 600 acres of soybeans and corn each spring. Clarence deftly handles Paul's four-wheel-drive tractor with a seven-bottom plow—bigger equipment than he operated before retiring. He also helps with harvest in the fall, trucking grain from the combine.

It's obvious that in the field or in the kitchen, Clarence Strater is a real blue ribbon farmer with a great appetite for life.

PRIDE OF IOWA COOKIES
("Pride of Grandpa" cookies)

    1 cup brown sugar
    1 cup white sugar
    1 cup shortening
    2 eggs
1/2 teaspoon salt
    1 teaspoon baking soda
    1 teaspoon baking powder
    2 cups flour
    1 teaspoon vanilla
    1 cup coconut
    3 cups quick-cook rolled oats
1/2 cup chopped nuts

Blend sugar and shortening, add beaten eggs. Sift dry ingredients together and add to first mixture. Stir in vanilla, coconut, oats and nuts. Mix well and drop by teaspoonfuls on greased cookie sheet. Flatten with bottom of glass. Bake until brown at 375° (about 8 minutes).

BUTTERMILK BREAD OR ROLLS

    1 cup buttermilk
    3 tablespoons sugar
2-1/2 teaspoons salt
    6 tablespoons shortening
    1 cup warm water
    1 package or cake yeast
    1 egg, beaten

1/2 teaspoon baking soda
    6 cups flour

Heat buttermilk. Stir in sugar, salt and shortening. Cool to lukewarm. Measure water into large mixing bowl (warm, not hot, water for active

TASTY TECHNIQUES. Apron slogan is family joke—Clarence puts pride into his pecan rolls, and they turn out perfect, batch after batch. And while oven's still warm, this cooking grandpa flattens sheet of cookies.

dry yeast; lukewarm water for compressed yeast). Sprinkle or crumble in yeast. Stir until dissolved. Add lukewarm milk mixture. Add beaten egg.

MMM—GOOD! Clarence has won lots of awards for cooking, but his biggest reward is smiles from family!

Combine baking soda and 3 cups flour. Add to yeast mixture and beat until smooth. Stir in remaining flour. Turn dough out on lightly floured bread board; knead until smooth and elastic. Place dough in a greased bowl; brush top lightly with soft shortening. Cover with a towel and let rise in a warm place, free from draft, until doubled in bulk, about 1 hour. Punch down and turn out on lightly floured board. Divide in half and shape into loaves or make up in rolls. Let rise about 1 hour again. Bake rolls at 400° for 15 minutes. Bake bread at 375° for 30 minutes, then turn to 325° for 30 minutes.

PECAN ROLLS

Melt 1/4 cup butter in a saucepan. Add 3/4 cup brown sugar and 2 tablespoons water, cook slightly and stir until sugar is melted. Pour in the bottom of greased pans or muffin cups. Scatter pecan pieces or halves over syrup. Roll dough to 1/4-in. thickness, spread with soft butter and sprinkle with cinnamon. Roll up and cut into 1-in. pieces. Place in syrup about 1 in. apart. Let rise about 1 hour and bake at 400° for 15 to 25 minutes. **Note:** This amount of syrup is for two 9-in.-round cake pans. Roll half of dough at a time.

To Almost Everyone, He's Just Plain 'Papa'!

By Tom Cooper

All through his many years of farming, Edward Wadsworth of Prattville, Alabama has been called a lot of things—all of them good.

Some folks say he's "Alabama's No. 1 farmer", others that he's the "best cattleman in America". But mostly his family, friends and the legion of people he's helped in his lifetime just call him "Papa".

Why? "Because so many people love him," his wife, Hope, explains simply.

Papa has willingly offered advice and assistance to countless fellow farmers over the years—raising the eyebrows of some who can't understand helping out a "competitor".

Papa just shakes his head at such a notion. "I can't think of a single reason why we farmers shouldn't share our knowledge and help each other," he says forcefully.

Ironically, though, this remarkable cattleman came close to never having any farming know-how to pass along …he almost wasn't a farmer!

Papa grew up on one of the most successful cotton farms in the state. Then the boll weevil came along and all but wiped out the thriving operation his father, J.A. Wadsworth, had built up near Prattville.

Discouraged, J.A. sent his three sons to the Univ. of Alabama, urging them to get a business education. Soon, however, the Great Depression made college an unaffordable luxury.

So Papa and his brothers—Jack and Leonard—returned to the family farm. "There weren't any jobs to be had, but we had Daddy's farm and a few mules, so we started farming. Truth is, farming was all any of us really wanted."

That was in 1932, perhaps the most difficult year ever to begin farming. Having learned from the past, the brothers quickly agreed they would need to diversify to survive.

It wasn't easy, but the plan worked. The farm broke even in 1933, made a small profit in 1934 and has been profitable every year since.

J.A. died in 1934, but not before he had the satisfaction of seeing his sons put the family farm back on the road to prosperity.

Papa himself soon started building a big reputation in cattle circles. He helped organize the Alabama Cattleman's Assn. in 1940 and was

"GRAND" PAPA! Hope and Papa enjoy chat with granddaughter (also named Hope). Why's farmer called Papa? "Because people love him," his wife says.

an officer of the organization for more than two dozen years.

Now nearly everyone who visits with Papa comes away proclaiming him the best farmer in all of Alabama. And no less an authority than John Armstrong, manager of the gigantic King Ranch in Texas, calls Papa the "best cattleman in America".

Papa scoffs at these accolades. "What I know about cattle comes from living with them for 50 years. If I deserve any of those nice titles, it's just because all my life I've listened more than I've talked!"

When it comes to listening, Papa's always had plenty of family nearby to bend his ear. When brother Leonard was married in 1936, the already close Wadsworths started becoming even closer—literally.

"There was plenty of room in our big house," Papa recalls, "so when Leonard married, he and his wife moved in with Mother, Jack and me. That worked so well that when Jack got married in 1938, he and his wife moved in. The next year Hope and I were married…and we moved in, too!"

Conditions may have been crowded, but the arrangement never caused any problems. In fact, for years the brothers owned only one car, rotating it among them.

It wasn't until 1948, after the birth of eight children, that the brothers decided it was finally time for each family to have a separate house.

Papa's brothers are gone now—Jack died in 1968 and Leonard in 1974—but the farm is still a family affair. Jack Jr., the only boy among the brothers' 10 children, now farms with his uncle.

And at 74, Papa has no plans to slow down. Most days he's working from first light, stopping only for a brief lunch (usually crackers covered with peanut butter, a banana and a Coke).

In fact, there's little that can keep Papa away from his cows for long. Recently,

HE'S THE BOSS. Papa has been called the best cattleman in America. After many years of farming, he has ready explanation: "Cattle can't talk back!"

44

hundreds of family and friends planned a party to honor him.

"Papa worked all morning out with his cattle," Hope smiles in recollection. "It wasn't until 15 minutes before the party was to start that he came in, just as unconcerned as you please. He took a shower, got dressed... and was ready on time!"

Papa is one man who's truly in love with his land and his livestock. "When Hope gets to fussing at me," he says, "I just get into my ol' Bronco and drive out to the pastures and look at my cows. It takes two to argue, you know...and my cattle don't talk back!"

All these years later, he hasn't a single regret over the way his life worked out.

There are greater financial riches in other lines of work, Papa allows. "But, I tell you," he adds without hesitation, "out here you get back to nature and God. This is the way things were created.

"I'm proud to be known as a farmer. We're feeding half the world."

Retirement? Papa just laughs. "As far as I'm concerned," he calls over his shoulder as he heads out to check his cattle, "the day I went into farming is the day I retired!"

GIVE AND TAKE is Papa's heartfelt belief. "Farmers should help each other," he says.

Old-Time Equipment Chugs Again at Antique Tractor Pull

By Gene Prigge

Avid tractor-pull fans looking for multi-engined monster tractors screaming, roaring and rumbling in front of the grandstand shouldn't come to the Hungry Hollow Steam and Gas Engine antique tractor pull.

This tractor pull, you see, is limited to machines built before 1939—complete with governors. (No...as old-timers remember, those aren't politicians. A governor is an old-fashioned gadget that kept steam-powered tractors from working so hard they blew up!)

In this unique event, memories are every bit as important as machines. For the past 14

years, a couple dozen gas- and steam-engine enthusiasts from western Wisconsin have been showing their collection each summer at the county fairgrounds at Rice Lake, Wisconsin. Last year, however, the Hungry Hollow Tractor Club decided to add a dash of excitement with a tractor pull...and brought back many fond recollections in the process.

Club members designated six weight classes—from lightweights under 3,200 lbs. up to an open class where two old Oil Pulls vied for glory at 6,200-plus lbs.

Since it wasn't an officially sanctioned event, the technical details of the pull weren't exactly scientific. The initial weight consisted of concrete blocks stacked "about up to here", one

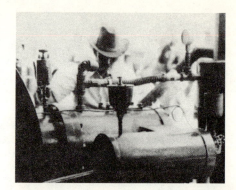

pull official reported, gesturing toward his knees.

After the tractors chugged away from the start, two people would jump onto the sled at 10-ft. intervals, until the weight was too much to pull.

One of the crowd favorites was 89-year-old Hans Anderson, a Rice Lake native. Hans brought his John Deere "G" tractor, bought new in 1929—one enthusiast said the well-preserved machine looked as if Hans had kept it in his living room!

Hans himself appeared to have come to the pull in his "Sunday-go-to-meetin'" clothes. He finished second, after his tractor divided time about equally between the field and repair shed.

Old John Deere "A" tractors seemed to be special favorites with spectators and owners alike, but the roster of entries also included such old-timers as Case, Moline, International Harvester, Oil Pull, Fordson and McDeering. Also on exhibition were Farmalls and Allis-Chalmers models, plus miscellaneous gas engines dating back to the turn of the century. Many of the old engines were put to work cutting wood, grinding wheat...even turning a popcorn popper!

Last year's event proved such a success with farm folks from miles around that the Hungry Hollow group plans to host antique tractor pulls every year. You might want to show up sometime if you're looking for a little action...and a ton of nostalgia!

OLD-TIME TRACTORS come out smokin', to the delight of the crowd—no one misses lack of power at this pull. Right, Hans Anderson readies '29 John Deere.

Justin Gordon: He's a Farmer, and Lots More

By his wife, Bernice Gordon

Someday I just knew that I would marry a man like Justin Gordon. When I was young and reached the "courtin'" age, I knew exactly what I was looking for, and Justin fit it to a "T".

I've now been married to him for 38 years, and he is still everything I admire in a man. He is kind, patient, understanding, caring and conservative...yet he has a spirit of adventure rumbling around inside of him that surfaces just often enough to keep you off balance.

He's led an interesting life and he loves to tell people about it. He has done everything from being an ice-man to riding the rails...and he rounded up wild horses out West in the days when there were no paved roads, few hotels and seldom enough money to go around.

By the time I met him he was a man of the world in the true sense of the word. He already had the ability to stand on his two feet without ever stepping on anyone else's.

Everybody—including me—loves to hear him tell his stories about those early years when he was rounding up wild horses in Montana, buying them from ranchers, homesteaders and sheepherders. Then they drove them to a railroad station at Miles City for shipment to Oak Harbor for the farmers of Ohio.

According to Justin (his friends all call him "J.J."), it was the law of the land then to welcome every traveler. And that law gave Justin some of his most unusual experiences—he stayed in log cabins, prospectors' shacks, dugouts and even sod houses which he calls "soddies".

You should see how quiet it gets when he starts telling about those days—he can spellbind any listener. He tells of the night they came on an old homesteader's cabin and the old fellow invited them in. There was nothing inside to sit on but a dirty cot and a tree stump.

The old guy sighed and said, "Grab a seat, boys. Ya know, the Bible says 'Ask and you shall receive'...and Teddy Roosevelt says 'Sit still and I'll bring it to you'. Shucks, I'm getting bed sores just layin' here waitin' for him."

Justin tells of another night when he stopped at a run-down cabin where the homesteader's wife had left him. The

WHITTLE WHILE. Justin still whittles with knife he first used when rounding up wild horses in Montana.

homesteader said, "Ya know, when I married her she was barefoot. I put shoes on her feet and she up and left me."

Our house is filled with laughter every time Justin starts telling about his experiences out West. But he has some stories about those days that aren't so funny, like the early blizzards and the axle-deep mud...and the depression and drought of 1936 when the government was paying $2.00 a head for sheep pelts, and he remembers seeing the range strewn with sheep carcasses as far as the eye could see as desperate people killed and skinned them...and the people ate mutton for breakfast, lunch and supper. Those were hard times.

It was during some of those lonely hours out on the range that Justin first began his whittling hobby, carving on any piece of wood he found out there. Today, over 50 years later, he's still using that same jackknife. The fact that he still has it is somehow indicative of his tenacity and thoroughness in anything he does.

Our boys have pretty much taken over our farming operation now, and on winter evenings, Justin once again has time to whittle his intricate carvings of things he recalls of his farming past. He's whittled things like an entire farmyard, complete with a barn and silo down to the smallest feeding trough, as well as a threshing machine, a steam engine, horse and buggies, etc.

He's whittled a lot more things, but he gives them away to family and friends. His collection is put on display from time to time so that the townspeople can enjoy a look into farming history in miniature.

Now don't get me wrong. Justin is far from retired. If he ever looks like he's standing still one of the boys says, "Hey, Dad, if you

HANDY HANDS! *Early farmstead above is among many whittling projects of Justin's.*

aren't doin' anything maybe you can give me a hand…" and he's off and running again.

In fact, he uses his bike to go from one farm to the other nearly every day, since the boys seem to have every available vehicle tied up "every darned time" he wants one. He laughs because the bike is a girl's model, and it doesn't have any brakes. But he says, thanks to all the space out here in the country, he has enough room to make a couple of big circles to slow it down before he stops in a field.

Of course, our grandchildren Sarah and little Justin keep him busy even during "slow periods". They think nothing is more fun than a tractor ride with Grandpa or going to feed his pet mules, Jack and Jenny. Yes, those two mules are dear to him—they're sort of a tie to the old days, as is the steam engine he recently bought and is trying to restore "just for fun".

I'd have to say all this was pretty predictable. In fact, our life style was predestined the day we got married, when I learned that his favorite wedding gift was a kid goat that was given to us by a friend who was one of Buffalo Bill's proteges.

A year later he bought a 73-acre farm on Jones Road in Penfield Township, Ohio, and our farming operation was launched, right here where we still live today.

The farm had a sturdy house and fairly good out-buildings, and a nice black walnut tree in the backyard. Naturally, there was no telephone, no paved roads, no furnace and no plumbing. We had one horse, one cow, a couple of calves, a few sheep and, of course, our "wedding goat". But Justin was happy—he was at home on *his* land.

The day we moved in, our new neighbors welcomed us with the dubious news that "no other farm family has ever made it on this farm" and that we probably wouldn't either. Justin just smiled and said, "Well now, we'll just see about that."

I knew by the set of his jaw that he'd decided right then and there that we *would* make it. We did—it's now 38 years later and he runs nearly 700 acres alongside Jones Road.

But it hasn't been easy. He worked dawn to dusk, 7 days a week, only taking out time to go to church. Many a night after supper I'd start

GRANDPA'S PRIDE AND JOY are Sarah and little Justin, held by Justin and Bernice above. Justin often commutes between his sons' farms on old bike at left—even though it doesn't have brakes!

looking for him and find he was out shocking corn in the moonlight.

He drove a milk truck and hauled cattle to supplement our income. It meant getting up at 4 a.m., walking through dew-soaked pastures to get the cows that always seemed to be in the farthest corner or hiding in the woods. He'd milk them and then be on the truck by 7 a.m.

About the only chance he had to rest was when the kids and I brought his lunch out to the fields. Then we'd all sit down and have a picnic under a tree or in the shade of the wagon.

We had five children—four boys and a girl. No matter how busy he was, Justin always managed to find time to play with them. Maybe it was because his own father had died when Justin was only 8, and from that experience he knew better than most men the value of a father.

Justin's strong character helped us all through the time our barn burned down in 1964. We were all so discouraged as we stood

and watched an entire season's hay go up in smoke, and heard our bull beller before it died, and realized that our sons' 4-H pigs were perishing in the flames.

Again there was that determined set to his jaw, and soon a new barn appeared outside my kitchen window. As often happens, some good comes out of bad, and so it was with the loss of our barn—the new barn sparked a surge of progress on our farm, with new facilities that allowed us to eventually increase from 30 to 175 head of cows.

Justin has always been ingenious, and much of his inventiveness has rubbed off on our sons. He's especially proud of the five-on-a-side milking parlor that's run by a touch of a switch—our boys designed and built the whole thing. Another thing that Justing thinks is pretty neat is the automatic feeder the boys built—it runs by an electro-magnet from our old Maytag washing machine.

He gets pleasure out of the simple things in life. He doesn't smoke or drink, but he does have one habit to which he's addicted: farm sales. Lord, does he love farm sales! It all started when we first needed some used horse-drawn equipment, and to this day he can't pass up a good farm sale. He seldom buys anything—he just enjoys watching the finagling and talking to the other farmers there.

When you ask Justin what he likes best about farming, he says, "The challenge. To plant in the spring and not know what you'll get. In the poor years, you just hope to get enough yield to pay for more seed so you can try again next year."

In every man's life, there is a time to plant and a time to harvest. I'm glad to see Justin slow down just a little now so he can enjoy the harvest that he's earned.

I've been married to him for 38 years, and he's still everything I admire in a man. Oh, sometimes I wish he wouldn't wear his patched overalls to town or wear his old straw hat when we have company, but he says that's just "woman pickin' ".

He's still looking at our place like he's just getting started in farming, planning more changes and looking ahead to the future. He's already replaced every one of our original farm buildings.

Only two things from those early years remain pretty much as they were—that nice black walnut tree, and Justin. Both have been weathered by summer sun and winter winds. But both are still standing strong.

PET MULES "Jack" and "Jenny" keep tie to old days for family. Above, Justin chats with his sons.

The 'Jolly Boys Club' Meets Only To Eat!

By Frank and Ada Yoder

The sign in the game room of Cooper's Cafe in downtown Wellman, Iowa says "NO FOOD OR DRINK IN HERE!" But once a month, this rule is waived for some heavy reasons. The game machines are shoved aside, tables are pushed together, and placemats set out. Owner Shirley Cooper crawls under the large tables leveling the legs with shims of paper. Then she checks all the chairs to make sure they're sound and sturdy.

Why? "Well," she explains in her friendly way, "the Jolly Boys are a-comin' to dinner today, and some of 'em are just a mite hefty. They come in for their 'monthly' meeting every so often, though there's really no set schedule. Those bumpkins couldn't live by schedules!"

And sure enough, one by one, the portly fellows start to drift in, examine their chairs and sit. Today the ex-mayor of Wellman, curly-haired, fortyish Duane Tadlock, is chosen as Master of Ceremonies, which immediately angers the only "charter member" of the group, Ralph Gingerich. The others good-naturedly cool him down with such sage reasoning as, "Tadlock's the only fellow from our group who's ever held public office, and we want him to talk today. Besides, you look a mite bleary-eyed."

Instead, 78-year-old Ralph is called on to relate the beginnings of the Fat Man's Club, as it was originally called when started some 25 years ago. "Well...we've had catfish from the Mississippi...moose...fried coon...turtle from the English River, as well as Rocky Mountain oysters, deer and salmon from Alaska. Ya, it's really a social affair."

By this time the food starts to arrive from the kitchen. There are tubs of brown gravy, sweet corn, peas and carrots, gobs and gobs of cottage cheese with onions and diced radishes, thick slices of brown and white bread, bowls of butter, gallons of coffee and the main entree— thick cut slices of smoked ham.

The room turns quiet as the anticipation for "digging in" grows, and someone says, "Marlowe, take off your hat!" A self-appointed chaplain offers a prayer of thanksgiving for the food, and then the Jolly Boys "belly up" with

A BUNCH TO MUNCH. This group doesn't do much talking—members usually have their mouths full! At right, Marlowe Mathes shows club's purpose.

elbows carefully poised on the table.

There's no conversation during the meal—only occasional calls for more coffee or seconds. Later, over huge slices of cream pies, the men reminisce.

"Yup," Ralph Gingerich says, "the very best of the best of this ol' farm town have been members of the Jolly Boys. Eddie Jones, Tiny Swartzendruber, Joe D. Yoder...and the list goes on and on."

How does one become a member? "It's by invitation only," Ralph explains. "We've agreed there'll be only 12 members, but beyond that we have no rules." Portly Ed Burkholder, a semi-retired farmer, adds, "We have no dues, and no projects. We meet to eat, and that's all."

After more coffee and chatter, chairs begin to scrape back as Duane Tadlock gathers in the $4.00 fee for the trimmin's, places it in his hat and heads for the cashier. The rest of the group sits around for a while longer, talking about farm prices, the weather and whatever else affects their respective jobs as farmers, lumber yard foreman, tank truck drivers. Finally they begin to drift out the door.

Two of them remain behind and watch

the club's only charter member—charter more by weight than tenure—crossing the street. "Ya know," says one, "there's a lot of sideways motion goin' on there, even when he gets to going straight-forward!"

One of the other old-timers slowly pushes his 200-plus pounds away from the wall he's been leaning against. "Well," he says to the other fellow with a satisfied smile, "see ya'all at the next meetin'."

WIDE LOAD. Cafe owner Shirley Cooper (right) checks to make sure chairs will hold before boys sit!

The 'Hilger Kids': They're Still Staying Young at Heart

By Roberta Donovan

Their combined ages total more than 200 years...but nearly everyone still calls them the "Hilger Kids". They're Babe Hilger, 65, and her "big brothers", Dan, 75, and Bryan, 71. And if you spend a day following these three around their sprawling Montana ranch...well, you just might begin to believe they really *are* kids.

Babe, Dan and Bryan have been known as the "Hilger Kids" ever since they were the young grandchildren of Nicholas Hilger, who founded the 10,000-acre ranch along the Missouri River in 1867.

And the Hilger Kids—who grew up on the ranch and never left—know every square foot of it, the way some folks know their living room.

"A man from the Polled Hereford Association once asked us if we ride it," Bryan recalls with a smile.

Babe chuckles. "We told him we sure do," she says. "It's a lot easier to ride 10,000 acres than it is to *walk* it!"

Babe doesn't ride just to check up on things. In fact, she admits she'd rather be on a horse than doing almost anything else.

"But I don't ride quite as much as I used to anymore," she says. "When my sister passed away, I lost my riding partner."

The Hilgers have always been a close-knit clan. None of the three Kids has ever married... "at least not yet," Bryan notes with a grin.

The scenic home they share nestles in Hilger Valley, about 18 miles north of Montana's capital city of Helena.

Little has changed since the days of Grandpa Nicholas. Oh, there's an interstate highway a mile or so away now, but the valley itself slumbers much like nearby Sleeping Giant Mountain. The Hilgers' ranch lies between the Big Belt Mountains to the north and the main range of the Rockies to the west.

Like in the days of Nicholas, Hilger Valley gets little snow or rain and is one of the driest spots in Montana. But despite lack of moisture, the Kids manage to raise horses and alfalfa...and fine cattle. The Hilgers' registered Polled Herefords are known by cattlemen all over the U.S. and even into Canada.

During winter, Bryan and Babe rely on a sleigh pulled by a team of horses to get feed to their cattle, and until recently Babe raked hay with draft horses.

"I enjoyed that," Babe recalls with a satisfied smile. "People driving by would stop and take pictures when I was raking near the highway. I was always happy to talk to them—a lot of people are too young to remember when *everyone* raked with horses."

The Hilgers now run about 75 cows on

BREW BREAK! Sister Babe calls in brothers for strong ranch coffee.

their ranch, along with a few replacement heifers, and put up about 250 tons of hay a year.

There's a good reason the Kids still do almost all the work around the ranch, according to elder brother Dan.

"It's hard to get anybody that will really work anymore," he explains. "Why, a lot of younger people can't handle ranch work—can't even seem to learn how to stack hay right!"

The Kids have lived through a lot of history. Their lives stretch back to a time when Indians camped in their isolated valley.

But, aware that an era can vanish as quickly as a memory, the Hilgers have converted an old stone house on the ranch into a small family museum. The Kids are always happy to show visitors through, proudly pointing out old scythes, bear traps, butter churns and other family treasures they've put on display.

When they can take time from ranching,

DO IT YOURSELF. There's no hired help on this spread—the "Kids" do it all. Babe, 65, rounds up cattle (below) then makes plans with brother Dan, 75.

that is. "Oh, we're getting a little slower," Bryan admits. Adds Dan, "To be honest, the mountains *do* seem a little higher than they used to!"

Partly because of that, this energetic trio will soon be slowing down a bit. They're now in the process of turning their ranch over to a

younger fellow…one who was carefully picked.

His offer was not the first—or the biggest—the Kids had for their ranch. Fact is, they had quite a few—but mostly from developers who wanted to turn Grandpa Nicholas' acres into subdivisions. The Kids turned down every one of those offers.

The ranch's new owner has promised he'll keep every acre part of a working ranch. So, after many long family talks, the Kids decided to pass the ranch on to him.

Grandpa Nicholas would approve of the way his Kids turned out!

STILL SPRY at 71, brother Bryan weighs in cattle (right) while Babe watches. The "Kids" admit their pace has slowed, so they're ready to pass ranch on.

Mule Skinner's Secret? A Treat and a Touch!

By Joan Hosman

Through all the years he farmed, Howard Sartain made sure of one thing: Each spring he took care to plant a little orange-top cane on his farm outside Fayette, Missouri. The cane was a special treat for his mules.

"Let my neighbors worry about gas for those big tractors of theirs," he'd snort to himself. "This is all the fuel I'll ever need."

In his 85 years of living on and farming the same farm, Howard never owned a tractor… and never had need to. Every year he'd harness up his mules and produce all the corn, hay and grass his growing cattle herd needed.

When most people think of the Missouri mule, the first word that comes to mind is "stubborn". But Howard's one farmer who's never forgotten all the mule contributed to early settlers of the Show Me State. "They're the ones that plowed and harvested the fields," he points out, "and built the railroads, too."

Howard's retired recently, but he still gives a daily grooming to a span of sorrel mules any mule lover would give his eyeteeth to own. And though his mules are nameless, he speaks their language.

"A mule isn't stubborn," he asserts, "unless his owner makes him that way."

Howard should know. He's spent nearly all his life around mules.

"Back in my younger days," he reminisces, "I boarded and broke mules to the harness so they could do the fieldwork for farmers around here. I've been a mule skinner a long time, since before I was 16."

Howard takes a backseat to no one in his regard for the mule. "Mules are a one-man animal," he states. "They like their work patterns the same, with no alterations. Just do that, and they'll outwork a horse any day."

But he also *understands* mules. "They've got a bit of mischief in them," he explains, "so there's only two places for a mule—in the harness or in the barn."

Over the years, Howard's sold more mules than most folks have seen. He's always been a fair but alert trader, and has often turned the tables on those few who thought they could take advantage of him.

"Once, I had two fellows come out to my farm to look over some of my finest mules," Howard recalls. "After they'd inspected 'em real close, they told me those mules just weren't up to par. 'They've got a knot on their hock,' they said.

"Next day," he adds, with a smile now beginning to play across his leathery face, "those same two fellows came back to buy the mules. 'Mister', they told me, 'you've probably heard

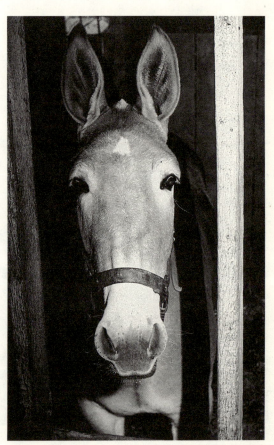

that mules went down $25 a head today.'

"I gave 'em a good long look. "Well, fellows,' I said, 'that may be true elsewhere. But around here mules just went *up* $25 a head.' I sold those mules—at *my* price!"

Today, Howard's cattle are gone from his farm...but the mules remain. And he treasures the pictures on his wall that show him farming with four proud mules in harness.

Mules are no mystery to this farmer. He knows all they need is a little orange-top cane...and a special touch.

STILL PULLING. Howard has slowed his pace, but mules still play a large role on his farm. Retired now, he enjoys spinning yarns with old mule skinner friends.

Elevated Farming!

"MY DAD's 89 now, but he's still going strong," says Bonnie Morgan of Zillah, Washington.

"Dad lives, as he has for 80 years, in the mountainous region of northern Idaho. Out there, there are but two directions—uphill and downhill!

"Anyway, Dad recently came to visit me in my little hideaway on the 'backside of the desert'. He scanned my land silently for a few minutes, then remarked, 'You folks around here waste too much ground. Where I come from, we stand it up on end—and farm three sides of it!' "

Farmer Sings 'Thank Heaven for Little Girls'!

Seven times Wisconsin dairyman Clarence "Cluck" Wolfe anxiously awaited the birth of his first son. But seven times his wife, Marge, gave birth to a bouncing baby girl.

Disappointed? No way. Cluck is almost never without a smile on his face. Blessed with a good disposition and a great sense of humor,

he's taken all of the chiding from his farm friends in stride.

In fact, when a neighbor teased him after the birth of his fifth daughter, Cluck retorted, "Heck, five of a kind beats a full house any day!"

He didn't know at the time that he'd soon have seven of a kind. Nor did he know that, out of his first 13 grandchildren, *11* of those would be girls, too!

Our contact with the Wolfe family began when Marge sent us a photo of their farm as an entry for *Farm & Ranch Living* magazine's "Prettiest Place in the Country" contest.

We felt a dairyman with seven daughters was rather unique, so we wrote back to her requesting more details on this bright, good-looking family.

Marge responded with the photos you see here, along with a letter, and we decided our readers would enjoy watching the Wolfe family "grow up", too.

Marge told us some other interesting things in her letter: "I was born in Milwaukee, a city gal, and met 'Cluck'—that's what he's always been called—on a manure spreader ride!

"See, I was visiting in his farm area, and he dared me as a young girl to ride with him on the tractor while he hauled a load of manure. He thought I was too 'stuck up' to do it, since I was from 'town'. But I took him up on it, and

that started our romance."

Well, Marge, many love stories have unusual beginnings, but we're sure your "manure spreader ride romanace" is more unusual than most!

Anyway, as the pictures indicate, the Wolfes proceeded to produce a virtual "harem", and the daughters have now continued the "tradition" by producing 11 more granddaughters! (Can you imagine the noise at the Wolfe household when that first grandson arrived???)

"It has been a wonderful life," Marge continued in her letter, "full and busy, but

DOTING DAUGHTERS *grew from tykes (top) to young mothers on Clarence Wolfe's dairy farm. Seven girls have produced 11 more female farmers for "Grandpa Cluck", smiling proudly center above.*

always lively." She reported that the girls have been highly appreciative of their home life and have shown it in many ways.

"For example, for our 25th wedding anniversary, Cluck surprised me with a trip to Hawaii, and our girls helped our hired man with all the milking and other farm chores while we were gone.

"And during another winter, one of our daughters came home from college to help so Cluck and I could take a trip to Florida—it was her way of saying 'thanks' for the opportunity to go to school.

"By necessity, all the girls have been a great help and became very good tractor drivers. Of course, they've had a super father, too."

Here's to you, Grandpa Cluck. You've proved that when it comes to daughters, seven is indeed a lucky number!

But Grandma— You're a Big Girl

"A FEW YEARS AGO we were visiting our son and daughter-in-law for a few days," Mrs. Chester A. Rogers of Carrollton, Ohio says.

"Our two grandchildren, Holly, 6, and Adam, 4, had just finished a bath and, dressed in fresh pajamas, ran to get their bed pillows.

"When Adam came into the living room with his pillow, I remarked, 'You know, Adam, Grandpa and I have pillowcases just like yours!'

" 'Really?' Adam said. 'Where does Grandpa sleep?'

" 'Grandpa sleeps with me,' I told him.

"Adam looked puzzled over that response. 'Gee, Grandma, why?' he demanded. 'What are you scared of?' "

He's Been Steady in the Saddle for Many Miles!

By Roberta Donovan

The distance between Swend Holland's "home ranch" and his sprawling summer range is about 65 miles, and he's ridden between the two places on horseback "since I was maybe 5 or 6 years old."

Ranching has always been part of his life —especially on these two places. His father homesteaded the "home place" ranch in 1892, and it has now grown to 8,500 acres. The distant summer range began being used by the family in 1895. Then, as now, trail drives were used to move the livestock over the 65-mile trek to the range each spring and back each fall.

"This range is attached to me like one of my arms," says Swend, making his saddle leather squeak as he shifts to scan the sagebrush-covered prairie. "I've never known anything but riding over this country."

But that doesn't mean that Swend has led a "sheltered" or uninteresting life. It takes only one evening of sitting around campfire with him during the fall roundup, listening to him drawl on in his colorful "cowboy patter" language, to learn that he's had some pretty exciting times out here in the "Big Sky Country" of central Montana.

Our conversation took place at the mid-point of the annual fall roundup. As Swend talked about his early days, he was sitting on a folding chair which he'd brought out of the sheep wagon. The chair was the one concession to modern conveniences at this line camp on his summer range. Otherwise, the camp is about as primitive and unchanged as it has been for years.

Its sole buildings consist of a sheep wagon where the cooking is done, a small homesteader's shack large enough for a couple of double-deck bunks, and—a little distance away—a small "one holer" with no door. It does, fortunately, face away from the other structures.

The camp is 12 miles from the nearest highway, and reached only by a rutted dirt road that is virtually impassable in wet weather. "I'd guess the nearest neighboring ranch is about 10 miles away," Swend says.

No power or telephone lines break the wide expanse of prairie here. In fact, it's so quiet that when Swend stops talking, you can sometimes hear a cow bawling to her calf a couple of miles away.

Furnishings are pretty simple in the canvas-topped sheep wagon behind us, now glowing from the flickering flames. Propane tanks provide fuel for cooking and refrigeration out here, and gasoline lanterns are used for light. Water is hauled to the camp in cream cans.

It's obvious Swend loves this old sheep wagon, which serves as both kitchen and "dining room". Folding chairs expand the number that can be seated around the old dining table.

The only cupboard—actually just some open shelves—holds everything from canned goods and dishes to dishtowels and pots and pans. Hanging from nails along the wall are a conglomeration of cast-iron skillets, mackinaws, cowboy hats and bridles.

"I never lock the door on the sheep wagon," Swend says. It's a long distance between places in this part of the prairie, and on more than one occasion, people stranded by a sudden storm have taken refuge here. Swend leaves it stocked with canned goods "just in case".

Those provisions could save someone's life, because there's no other shelter in sight for miles in any direction. This summer range includes several thousand acres of deeded land, plus leased state and federal land, all largely untouched from when herds of buffalo roamed here. To give you an idea of the vastness of this range, Swend's holding pasture alone contains 6 sections of land!

For Swend, the annual fall roundup is a nostalgic time of year when he recalls nearly 50 years of "cowboying" and sleeping under the

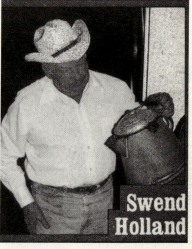

Swend Holland

stars. "It used to get cold in those bedrolls—really cold. I can remember waking up and finding all kinds of frost near your face that had been formed from your breath during the night.

"That hot 'gunboat' coffee in the morning served by the camp cook worked almost like anti-freeze! And we always had sourdough hotcakes for our outfit every morning. That was something you could be as certain of as the sun coming up."

Swend's family ran sheep on this range when he was a "young'un", and he spent a lot of time helping the cook. As a result, he picked up a knack for cooking which he still has today.

"Keeping a sourdough starter was highly important in those days," Swend says. "You'd protect it with your gun if you had to. You couldn't run to the corner store for a package of yeast then, so sourdough starter was the only way to leaven bread or make hotcakes."

A sourdough starter is exactly what the name implies. Flour and water are mixed into a soft dough formation and allowed to sour, or ferment, at room temperature.

The night before it's used, additional flour and water are added to make up for that which will be used the next day. When it's time to make hotcakes or bread, part of the starter (Swend calls it the "heel") is carefully set aside to save it for the next time.

Nowadays this starter can be stored in the refrigerator for several weeks. But in the early days, it was kept on the back of the old kitchen range and used every day to keep it from getting too sour.

"If you missed using it a day or two," Swend says, "it would get a little strong. It might even scare some people, but it gave the hotcakes a good flavor.

"The rule of thumb, handed down by generations of sourdough cooks, was 'If the starter turns orange, it's still okay; but if it turns green, throw it out'."

Swend says every precaution was used to protect the starter in the early days. On a bitterly cold winter night, it wasn't unusual for the cook to put the sourdough in a bag and take it to bed with him to keep it from freezing.

And when traveling in cold weather, cowboys and mountain men would often put some sourdough starter in an old Prince Albert tobacco can and tuck it in the pocket of their wool shirt. Others simply put the starter in a bag around their neck and hung it inside their shirt to share any body warmth.

At any rate, a gift of a starter to someone along the trail who didn't have one was considered a real mark of friendship.

Swend, whose love of cooking comes second only to his love of ranching, believes in good, plain food. "To keep our cowboys happy when we're out working cattle, it's generally lots of meat, potatoes and gravy," he says, "especially in the evening. There's nothing better than a good meal after a hard day's work.

"Sometimes we eat breakfast a couple of hours before daylight, and it might be after dark before we eat our second meal. These young fellows get pretty hungry, so I give them all they want—just like the army, trailriders travel on their stomach."

Swend downed the last swallow of his sturdy, boiled "gunboat" coffee, and rose to his feet. "Time to hit the hay," he said. "That ol' haymaker of a sun is going to be rising before we know it, and we got a lot of critters to move in the morning."

With that, he shuffled off to the homesteader's shack. It was obvious—though he was tired—he was looking forward to being back in the saddle in the morning, after "whuppin' up" another hearty breakfast for his crew of cowboys.

WIDE OPEN SPACES is what Swend loves, and he has plenty of it. His sprawling summer range is 12 miles from nearest highway. Below are only buildings on range—cook's wagon, shack and privy.

These Grandpas Keep Old Depot on Track!

By Herm Nathan

The trains that rumble through the small town of Lancaster, Texas these days no longer pause at the weather-beaten old "Katy" depot. In fact, the last train stopped there more than 10 years ago. But from the activity at the depot this afternoon, you'd think a whole trainload of freight crates was due any minute!

Outside a half dozen cars and pickups are parked; inside the murmur of voices and laughter floats from the depot on hot Texas winds. Standing in the doorway, you can see a group of seasoned gentlemen intently hunched over a heavy wooden table, worn in the center from hard usage.

These grandpas—farmers, ranchers, former railroad men and town folks—gather at the depot every afternoon and Saturday morn-

ing. They debate this and that, talk fishing, chew tobacco and swap yarns. But, mainly, they spend their time on the serious business of playing dominoes!

Dominoes? "It gives us all something different to do," 80-year-old Charlie Miller explains in a gruff voice as he waits his turn at the "bones". "Besides, I can't just hang around the house all the time."

How Lancaster's venerable old railroad depot became the preserve of the town's domino-playing grandpas is a story in itself.

For years, the trains of the Missouri-Kansas-Texas Railroad ("Katy" for short) regularly brought freight to the depot, opened in 1889. But the trains stopped stopping at Lancaster a decade ago...and railroad officials decided to tear down the baggage and telegraph office station.

That seemed simple enough...but they didn't reckon with the folks of the town. Within 3 days of the railroad's announcement that it would demolish the depot, residents had raised $7,000 to save it—and a part of their heritage.

The Lancaster Historical Society purchased the depot from surprised railroad officials with part of the money and planned to turn it into a town museum. But the old building turned out to be too much of a fire hazard for that use.

So 2 years ago the Historical Society gave the domino players free use of the depot—and

STILL HUMMING! Lancaster, Texas' old railroad depot (opposite) has been turned into a busy domino parlor by grandpas like E.A. "Mug" Douglas (above).

it's been a beehive of activity ever since.

"I play dominoes for the sport of it and for the pastime," 84-year-old E.A. "Mug" Douglas says as he impatiently waits his turn. "In fact, this is my *only* hobby!"

Hobby actually is a tame word for the battles waged here—these fellows take their dominoes seriously! But in between games there's time to admire the details of this unusual domino parlor.

Things look pretty much like they did when the depot was new almost a century ago. There are antique gas lamps (now wired for electric current), a potbellied stove, a wooden tongue-and-groove ceiling and—jutting above the roof—a semaphore tower, ready to flag down passing freights…or the memories of them.

What's in the domino depot's future? Well, there's been talk around Lancaster of adding a kitchen and turning the building into a community hall. The regulars at the depot aren't so sure about that idea.

"I'm happy with it just as it is," declares 65-year-old Rosie McDonald. And the others are quick to agree with him.

For them the old-fashioned railroad depot is just the ticket for exciting competition and warm companionship. The trains may speed right by them as they play—but when it comes to sharing fun with old friends, they have no trouble getting aboard!

MAKING A MOVE, John B. Docker shows how seriously these Texans take their dominoes! But there's also time to enjoy unique "parlor".